THE EARLIEST DUTCH VISITS TO CEYLON

THE EARLIEST DUTCH VISITS TO CEYLON

DONALD FERGUSON

GYAN

Published by

Gyan Publishing House
5, Ansari Road
Daryaganj, New Delhi-110002
Phone: 011-47034999, 9811692060
E-mail: books@gyanbooks.com

Distribution Network
gyanbooks.com
India, USA, Canada, UK, Australia, France

ISBN : 978-81-212-4516-6 (HB)
First Published, Calombo, 1927-1930

2nd Impression 2020

Printed at: Gyan Press, Delhi.

THE EARLIEST DUTCH VISITS TO CEYLON

BY DONALD FERGUSON.

That the first visits of the Dutch to Ceylon, 1601 and 1602, were not accidental but pre-arranged is certain ; and there can be no doubt why Matecalo was the place to which Spilbergen's ships directed their course[1]. In 1598 two ships, the *Leeuw* and *Leeuwin*, owned by Balthazer de Moucheron[2] of Vere in the island of Walcheren, left Flushing for Achin under the command of Cornelis de Houtman. John Davis, who was pilot on board the *Leeuw*, has left us an account[3] of that unfortunate voyage, which culminated in the capture by the Achinese of the *Leeuwin* and some smaller vessels, the death of Cornelis de Houtman and the imprisonment of his brother Frederik, and the loss by death or captivity of over sixty of the Dutch. The *Leeuw* having set out on her homeward voyage called at the Nicobar Islands for much needed provision, but could obtain no rice, which was the chief requisite. Thereupon, Davis tells us,

> The sixteenth (November 1599) wee departed shaping our course for the Ile Zeilon[4]. for wee were in great distresse, especially of Rice.
>
> The sixt (December) by God's great goodnes wee tooke a ship of Negapatam, which is a Citie in the Coast of Coromandell, shee was laden with Rice bound to Achien. There were in her threescore persons, of

1. See note 24 below.
2. He was head of the mercantile house of the Moucherons at Vere, being of French origin. (For further details see Hakluyt Society's edition of the *Voyages and Works of John Davis*, Introd. lxiv, and 133 n. l.) Davis calls him " Mushrom."
3. First printed by Purchas in his *Pilgrims*, bk. II, pt. I, and reprinted, with notes by Capt. A. H. Markham, in the volume named in the previous note, pp. 129-56. See also the *Travels of Pedro Teixeira* (Hac soc.), Intrdo. lxii-lxvi.
4. Davis does not say why Ceylon was chosen as the place where they hoped to get rice : perhaps the natives of Nicobar had advised the Dutch to go there.

Achien, of Java, of Zeilon[5], of Pegu, Narsinga[6], and Coromandel. By these people wee learned that in Zeilon there is a Citie named Matecalou, a place of great Trade[7], and that there wee might load our ships with Sinamon, Pepper and Cloves[8]. They also said that in Zeilon were great store of precious stones and Pearles: that the Countrey doth abound with all kind of Victuals, and that the King is an exceeding Enemie to the Portugals,[9] they also told us of a Citie named Trinquanamale, where was the like Trade.[10] So they promised to lade our ships, and royally to victuall us, for little money. Thereupon we laboured by all possible meanes to recover[11] the said places, but could not, for the wind was exceeding contrary. Then these Indians told us that if we would stay untill January, we should have more than a hundred ships come close by that shore laden with Spicerie Linnen-cloth,[12] and China Commodities; besides stores and other wealth. To stay there as a man of Warre our Governour[13] would not agree: but to stay and in taking any thing to pay for the same he was content, for

5. Not Sinhalese, but probably Moorish traders.

6. Vijayanagar (see *Hobson-Jobson* s.v. 'Narsinga').

7. That the place had a consderable trade is evident from what we read in the journals that follow: this was probably owing to the fact that Matecalo was the port whence Kandy obtained its supplies (*of* C. A. S. Jl. xx. 127, 252 m 3). We know little of it before the Dutch visited it, the Portuguese writers rarely referring to it: the earliest to mention it, as far as I know, is Barros (see C. A. S. Jl. xx. 35).

8. The mention of cloves is obviously an error: certainly none would be got at Matecalo, unless from vessels that had come from the clove islands in the Eastern Archipelago.

9. Of the journals of Spilbergen Bree, &c., below.

10. Of Trincomalee as a trading port we learn nothing from Portuguese writers, but the statement here made seems to be justified by the statement of Captain Antonio Martins (see below, F 2, note 4.)

11. That is, reach, which meaning is now obsolete.

12. Meaning cotton.

13. Guyon Lefort. He had been the treasurer on board the *Leeuw* was captured by the Achinese, but was sent back with a message from the King to the Dutch, and so escaped captivity Cornelis de Houtman being killed, and the man appointed by sealed letter to succeed him having shared the same fate, a second sealed letter was opened, in which Lefort was named. Davis calls him the "sonne of Lafort a French Marchant dwelling in Seething-Lane." In the Spilbergen voyage of 1601 he commanded the *Ram*. (see further infra, B 1, note 7a.).

so was his Commission. To this the Company would not agree. Whereupon the eight and twentieth hereof we shaped our course homeward, having beaten sixteene dayes upon this Coast to recover Matecolou. We discharged our Prise the eighteenth hereof, having taken the best part of her Rice, for which our chiefe payed them to their content. But the Companie tooke away the Money and Merchandise from the Indians with much disorder: we tooke with us twelve of the Indians of severall places:[14] who after we could a little understand them, told us that the Merchants had great store of precious stones in the ships, which they had hid under the Timbers. Of what truth that report is I know not. They would not suffer Master Tomkins[15] nor me to goe aboord the Prise: for what reasons I know not.

On the 29th of July, 1600, the *Leeuw* arrived at Middelburg; and we may be sure that among other matters related by Guyon Lefort to Moucheron was the report of the Indians in the Negapatam ship regarding Matecalo and its trade. The shrewd merchant, recognising the importance of the information, determined to act upon it, and to despatch another fleet to Achin, which was, however, to call at Ceylon on the way. But at this time Moucheron had fallen into bad odour with the States-General, the Admiralty, and his fellow merchants; and a rival company had been formed, under the leadership of Adriaan Hendriksz ten Haeff, and including several of Moucheron's former partners.[16] This new company seems to have got an inkling of the information brought by Lefort, and to have resolved to forestall Moucheron. At any rate, the fleet of four ships despatched by this Zealand company on 28 January, 1601 for Achin called at Ceylon on its way thither to inquire regarding on opening for trade. Of this the pioneer visit of the Dutch to Ceylon we have scanty information, even the name of the place at which

14. What became of these men ultimately we do not learn.
15. Another Englishman serving on the *Leeuw*.
16. See de Jonge, *De Opkomst van het Nederlandchd Gezag in Oost Indië* I. 114 et seq.

the ships made landfall being unknown to us.[17] No result accrued from this visit, the natives, for some reason, assuring the strangers that no profit in trade was to be made there, and their assertion being too readily accepted.

Meanwhile Moucheron had got his fleet ready, consisting of three ships, the *Schaep*, the *Ram*, and the *Lam*, the first being commanded by Joris van Spilbergen, one of his trusted captains,[18] who was also admiral, the vice-admiral, on the *Ram*, being the same Guyon Lefort of whom we have read above. Owing to the very friendly relations existing between himself and the Prince of Orange,[19] Moucheron was able to obtain from the latter a friendly letter to the unknown monarch of Ceylon, of which Spilbergen was to be the bearer the admiral being also empowered by the prince to promise the Sinhalese king all the help he might need against his Portuguese enemies.[20] The three ships sailed from Vere on 5 May, 1601, thus only some three months after the departure of their rivals but, owing to delays on the voyage,[21] it was not until 31 May, 1602 that the *Schaep*, having lost one of her consorts near the Cape of Good Hope[22] and the other off the Comoro Islands,[23] cast anchor in the roadstead

17. See A. It is strange that no Dutch writer, as far as I knows has referred to this visit: even de Jonge (op cit.) passes it over in silence.

18. See de Jonge m.s., and if *The East and West Indian Mirror* (Hakluyt Soc.) Introd. xxxv et seq. The editor of this work hold, that "Speilbergen" is the correct spelling. I have preferred to retain the ordinary form.

19. See de Jonge u.s.

20. See infra, B 1.

21. For the causes see de Jonge u.s.

22. The *Ram*. She arrived at Matecalo on 3 July (see infra, B 1, s.d.).

23. The *Law*. She did not attempt to make Ceylon, but went direct to Achien (see infra, B 1).

of Matecalo.[24] Where exactly this was, I do not know but it must have been not far from Karativu.[25] It certainly was nowhere near the present Batticaloa,[26] as so many writers on Ceylon have erroneously stated. It is not my intention to give here an account of Spilbergen's doings in Ceylon: they have been told in brief by many writers, and as the relation of them by his diarist is hereafter given in full, a summary is needless. I shall only say that the *Schaep* and the *Ram* sailed from Ceylon on 3 September, arriving on the 16th at Achin, where they found their consort the *Lam*.

Meanwhile in Holland had been formed, on 20 March 1602, a General East India Company one of the first acts of which was to despatch to the East a fleet of 15 vessels, under the supreme command of Wybrand van Warwijck, the vice-admiral being Sebald de Weert.[27] The former left for Bantam with 12 vessels on 17 June, 1602, Sebald de Weert having already sailed, on 31 March, with three ships for Achin, but with orders to call at Ceylon on the way. Accordingly we find that de Weert cast anchor in Matecalo roadstead[28] on 28 November, less than three months after Spilbergen's departure therefrom. Of his visit to Kandy

---

24. It is surprising that such a careful scholar as de Jonge should commit a number of extraordinary errors in describing Spilbergen's arrival at Ceylon. He says (op. cit. ii. 275):—"He appears now to have been carried by the tide into the Indian Ocean above the Maldives (?), then along the coast of Cochin (?), and finally to have arrived on the west coast of Ceylon (?). Here all the coast-towns were occupied by the Portuguese, and he had no other choice but to double Point de Gale, and once more ply northwards to the east coast of Ceylon (!). On 31 May 1602 Spilbergh appeared in the roadstead of Matticalao (Sic) or Batticaloa (!), where some time later his admiral joined him." W. Van Geer (*De Opkomst van het Nederlandsch Gezag over Ceilon*, 12 n.), in pointing out de Jonge's error as regards the arrival at Matecalo road being due to chance, himself falls into several errors.

25. See notes to journals, &c. below.

26. That is, the town on Puliyantivu, which had its origin in the fort built in 1627 or 1628 by the Portuguese, who called it "Batecalou." see G 2, note 38). As regards the position of the town of "Matecalo" see infra, G 2, note 24.

27. He was one of the commanders in the disastrous expedition of June 1598 under Jacques Mahu and Simon de Cordes which attempted to circumnavigate the globe by the Magellan Strait, and was the only one that survived and reached home.

28. The reason why de Weert went direct to this place is not quite evident (see D 2, note 15).

and intercourse with Vimaladharma de Weert has left a very vivid and entertaining description, which will be found among the documents I have translated. I shall not attempt to summarize it here, as it deserves to be read in its entirety. I would only mention that Vimaladharma was urgent with de Weert, as he had been with Spilbergen, that the Dutch should come in force to Ceylon to help him to expel his enemies the Portuguese from the island, in return for which they were to have every facility for trade and be allowed to hold a fortified position on the sea-coast. Having previously despatched two of his ships to Achin, de Weert sailed for that port on 14 January 1603, arriving there on 5 February.

This visit to Ceylon had fired de Weert's imagination, and in the letter to his admiral quoted below he formulated a scheme for the occupation of Galle by the Dutch, with a twofold object : first, in order to have a central entrepôt for trade, and second, to do as much harm as possible to Portuguese ships going eastward or westward, all of which had to sight the point of Galle. After despatching this letter de Weert sailed once more, early in the morning of 3 April, 1603, for Ceylon, having now, in addition to his own three ships, three of van Warwijck's and a yacht. He also took with him an ambassador[29] from the Sultan of Achin to the King of Kandy. Owing to bad weather it was not until 25 April, that this fleet reached Matecalo roadstead where it cast anchor. Of this second visit of de Weert's to Ceylon we have two accounts by participants in the expedition,—one a very full and detailed narrative, the other a brief description, but none the less of value and interest. Both will be found further on. On his arrival de Weert lost no time in despatching a messenger to apprise Vimaladharma of the fact. The latter was, however, at the time in the western low-country waging war on the Portuguese and driving them out of their strongholds. He sent word to de Weert urging him to come with his ships as speedily as

29. Confusion regarding this man has led to the invention of an absurd story, elaborated by Baldaeus (see F 5 below), to account for the subsequent massacre.

possible to Galle and besiege it by sea, while he himself would attack it with his forces by land. The king also intimated his desire to meet de Weert at Vintare. In reply Vimaladharma was informed that the second wish could not be acceded to ; but it was resolved to proceed to Galle at the first opportunity. Meanwhile the Dutch spent their time in trying to push trade in various places ; and they also captured and plundered several Portuguese vessels that happened to be passing. When the king heard of this capture he was delighted, and wrote urging de Weert on no account to release the Portuguese prisoners. The vice-admiral had, however, pledged his word to the latter, and accordingly let them go. On 30 May word was received that the king would arrive next day at Matecalo, and accordingly on the 31st every preparation was made to receive him on board and on shore, a handsomely decorated tent being erected on the beach for the reception of His Majesty.

On 1 June de Weert landed with an armed force of 200 men, and met the king outside Matecalo. The meeting was cordial and the two parties proceeded to Matecalo. Here the king requested that de Weert should send his men back to the ships until next day, while the vice-admiral and a few companions should stay the night on shore. Of what followed we have a number of conflicting accounts, nearly all founded on hearsay. Only one writer, a captive Spanish officer, was an eye-witness ; and from his account I think there can be no doubt that while the king and de Weert were feasting, the latter, having drunk too much of the wine that he had had brought ashore, grossly insulted Vimaladharma. The king, already angry and suspicious with regard to the release of the Portuguese vessels, gave orders to bind the intoxicated vice-admiral, and the latter resisting was killed, though not by the king's command apparently. Then began a general massacre, many of de Weert's men, who, against orders, had gone into the various taverns thereabout, being killed outright or grievously wounded. Altogether some fifty Dutch lost their lives in this tragic affair.

During the next few days letters passed, under a flag of truce, between the king and the Dutch, the former disclaiming all responsibility for the massacre, and expressing his willingness for a renewal of friendly relations. Negotiations went on for some time, the king having meanwhile returned to Kandy ; and trade was also resumed with the inhabitants, but eventually, despairing of any useful issue, Jacob Pietersz, de Weert's successor, having already despatched two ships to Achin and one to Bantam, himself sailed for the former place with the rest of the fleet from Matecalo roadstead on 30 July, 1603.

Thus ended disastrously the first Dutch visits to Ceylon and intercourse was not renewed with the island by the Hollanders until 1610-12, when various treaties were entered into by the Dutch with Vimaladharma's successor, Senerat. Details of these and subsequent events will be given in a later paper.

ANNEXURES.

A. —The earliest visit of Dutch ships to Ceylon.
B1.—Extracts from the Spilbergen Journal.
B2.—Extracts from letter of Dutch Merchants at Achien.
C. —Extract from letter of Sebald de Weert.
D1.—Extract relating to de Weert's second visit to Ceylon.
D2 —Extract from Bree's Diary.
D3.—Extract from Rijcks's Diary.
E. —First visit of Dutch ships to Columbo.
F1. to 6.—Various extracts relating to de Weert's second visit and Massacre.
G1.—Extracts from Linschoten's "Reys-Gescrift.".
G2.—Rijklof van Goens on the Batticoloa and Panáma Territories.
G3.—Extract from Imray's *Indian Ocean Pilot*.

A.—THE VISIT OF DUTCH SHIPS TO CEYLON IN AUGUST, 1601.[1]

On the 14th August following,[2] the ships anchored before the island of Celon ;[3] and understanding from the people of that country that no profit was to be made there in respect of trade,[4] they pursued their voyage to the town of Achin in the island of Sumatra, being the destined place.[5]

---

1. The following extract is from a document, printed by de Jonge, *Opkomst van het Nederlandsch Gezag* ii 484-96, entitled "Short report, delivered by and on behalf of the company of Zealand, trading in the East Indies, whereby the hon mighty gentlemen the States General will be able to understand what passed during the voyage of the four ships fitted out by them, named, the one *Zeelandia*, of 300 lasts burden, Captain Cornelis Bastiaens, the other *Middelborch*, of 200 lasts burden, Captain Hans Huybrechtss Tonneman, the third the *Langhebereque*, of 150 tons burden, Captain Nicolaes Antheunissen, and the last the *Sonne*, of 70 tons burden, Captain Cornelis Adriaensz, whereof are returned the two ships, namely, *Zeelant* and the *Langhebereque*, the other two are still remaining on their voyage." The four vessels named sailed from Holland on 28th Jan, 1601, and arrived at Achin on 23rd August following. The *Zeelandia* and *Langhebereque* left Achin on 29th Nov., 1601, and arrived in Holland on 6th July, 1602. The other two ships did not reach home until the end of May, 1603. (see de Jonge, op, cit, ii. 252-9).

2. 1601, thus more than nine months before the visit of Spilbergen.

3. This vagueness is annoying; but, as the south-west monsoon must have been still prevailing, the place called at was doubtless on the east coast of Ceylon but not the roadstead of Matecalo apparently.

4. Fear of the Portuguese perhaps inspired this statement on the part of the natives, or possibly interested motives on the part of Muhammadan traders.

5. As mentioned in note 1, the ships reached Achin on 23rd August, 1601. By the *Zeelandia* and *Langhebereque*, which sailed for home on 29th November, there went to Holland two ambassadors from the King of Achin, one of whom died on 3rd August, 1602 in Middelburgh, where he was buried, a Latin epitaph being inscribed on his tomb (see Valentyn, *Sumatra* 29-30). The other envoy with the suite returned to Achin in 1603-4 (see infra, E, note 12).

B.—THE VISIT OF SPILBERGEN TO CEYLON IN MAY, 1602.[1]

The 23rd May (1602) we arrived at the altitude of 9½ degrees, very nearly opposite to Cochien on the coast of Malabre.[2] Fearing that we might meet with some storm and so be driven upon a lee shore,[3] we again proceeded somewhat more southerly in order to weather the Capo de Camorin, which we saw on the 26th ditto it was low land with a round hill We took note of a sign of many small black seamews with white heads, and so set our course for Poincto de Gallo,[4] the point[5] of the island of Celon, which we saw on the 28th ditto, and so sailed onward along the land of Celon,[6] and saw the first and second shoals[7], which we passed on the 29th. and had everywhere good ground of about twenty fathoms, and so sailed towards the river of Matecalo,[8] but first seeing a bay where seemed to be a river, we ran in towards it. Coming to the land on the 30th ditto, we saw that there was no river there, but found a great thicket of *Coques*[9]

1. In the *Ceylon Literary Register* vi. 308 et seq. I gave a translation of this narrative; but, as there were errors in it and in some of the footnotes, I have thought well to give a fresh translation, in which I have retained the spelling of proper names and strange words as found in the original, but have revised the faulty punctuation. I have followed the text of the first extant edition (1605) of the Journal of Spilbergen's voyage, pointing out in notes some variations in later editions. For information regarding these editions, and a summary of the whole of the voyage as given by Valentyn, see *C. Lit. Reg.* vi 308-10.

2. In the "Order of Plates" &c. in the first edition this is corrected to "Mallabar."

3. The south-west monsoon being then in full force.

4. In ed. of 1617 "Ponto de Galle."

5. In orig. "hoeck." cf. "Hook of Holland."

6. On the map *three* ships are shown near "Ponto de Galle," underneath them being the statement "Here the land was first sighted by us: we sailed forward to Matecalo." The course of each ship is marked by a dotted line.

7. The Great and Little Basses: see infra, G 1, notes 13, 15.

8. The word "riviere" in the original signifies a navigable river. On arriving off Matecalo the voyagers found that there was no river there (see *infra*), and that they had been misled by the sailing directions in Linschoten's *Reys-Geschrift* (see infra, G 1, note 44), which they evidently carried as their guide.

9. In ed. of 1617 "coquos."

trees, and saw a village wherein stood a *pagode*.[10] Coming to anchor there and sending our boat to land, they of the country came in a canoe to speak with our people and we asking them about Matecalo, they told us that it was yet more northerly; they also were able to name to us Capelle de Frerro.[11] We presented them with some knives: they promised to give us people the next day to bring us to Matecalo, the which took place on the 31st ditto, and we let a man go overland to Matecalo to speak to the king, who is named Dermuts Iangadare.[12] The same evening we came into the roadstead of Matecalo, which is a bay, where they build many ships,[13] and the king has his town a mile from there;[14] we heard of no river there, except about six miles further on, and it is a very dry river, where is scarcely 5 or 6 feet of water.[15]

The 1st of June came some Indians on board (the which nation is Cingales), bringing with them an interpreter who could speak Portuguese. They said to us that they had pepper and cinnamon enough, and that the *modeliar* (the king's captain on land) was desirous that the general should come on shore to speak with him. At the same time came back again our man whom we had sent to the king, and brought us the same tidings that there was pepper and cinnamon enough: the king had also received and entertained him well. The Cingales with their interpreter were presented with pretty glasses and other pretty things, and so went again on shore.

---

10. Probably the village and temple of Tirukkovil (see infra, note 141).

11. Capello de Frade (Friar's Hood): see infra, D 3, note 3, G 1, note 18).

12. The "king" was, of course, only a disáva or vanniya (see infra, G 2) and the name here given apparently represents Tamil *dharmaccangattiyar* (? friend of religion). Perhaps this is the same man described by Boshouwer in 1612 (see Baldaeus, *Ceylon*, chap. xi). as "Jaune Sangati, prince and lord of Podere" (? Porativu).

13. Bree and Rijcks do not mention this fact.

14. See the statements of Bree and Rijcks infra.

15. The distance mentioned (say 24 miles English) shows that the (modern) Batticaloa "river" is meant (see infra, D 2, note 99)

The 2nd ditto the general went on land with three or four men, where five elephants stood ready, which performed much ceremony in kneeling, and some also with their trunk took a man and set him on their body[16] : these elephants are very subtle and are well trained[17] in everything. These elephants of Celon are considered the most intelligent of the whole of India. The general coming to the aforesaid *modeliar* was well received and entertained; he promised to come the next day in order to go and visit the king at Matecalo.

The 3rd ditto the general again went on shore with divers presents to offer to the king; he took certain musicians with him that could play on divers instruments. Meanwhile there came aboard a canoe with a nobleman coming six or eight miles from the north,[18] desiring that we would come there with our ships but they of Matecalo were much against this, so that each one sought to persuade us in order to derive profit therefrom.

The 4th ditto the general let us know in writing that he would come with the king on to the shore.

The 5th ditto the general came again to the shore in the evening with the king, who was accompanied by some 1,000 men all armed. The general begged leave to come on board, who related to us what had befallen him. On first coming to Matecalo he was received by some principal lords, and was brought before the king, who had a guard of more than six hundred men with their naked weapons in their hands, and the king himself with a naked sword standing bade the general welcome, who there gave him divers presents; and thereafter, having heard the music and other instruments (which well pleased the king), he caused the general to be brought into the house of his *modeliar*, where he with his servants was well entertained. The next day the general was bidden to remain in his lodging with his people; towards

---

16. On the map an elephant is depicted doing this, not at Matecalo but between "Alicam" (Alutgame) and "Ponto de Galle."

17. In the 1605 edition after "wordèn" (are) comes "wonder," which appears to be the same word repeated by a printer's error in a transposed form. The ed. of 1617 omits "worden," but retains "wonder," which makes no sense.

18. This was doubtless an emissary from the headman of Palukamam (see infra, D 2, note 37).

the evening he was brought before the King, when it was strongly laid to his charge that he was a Portuguese, and with great difficulty did he make them believe otherwise, so that he again obtained his freedom to be able to go everywhere, so that the next day he came on board, as has been related above. Remaining on board that evening, he meanwhile entertained the king with other presents, and sent other persons on shore, seeking to treat the king with all friendship and gifts, in order that he might obtain his lading, which the king promised to give him in fifteen days.

The 6th June in the morning the general again went on land to the king, who received him by the shore, and at every moment was joined by more men with arms. The request of our general was all for lading. The king with great promises said that in five days he should have the larger half, and begged much that the ship should be discharged and the goods brought on land; many men and elephants had been sent there to carry the cargo. It was also asked by the *modeliar* to bring the ship up on to the shore, as they do their ships. This improper request of the *modeliar* caused our general a great suspicion that their actions rested on deceit. The general also learnt through some Moors and Turks that there was little or no pepper, because these people do not trade in it there; so that the general consented to what they requested and sought, to bring the ship upon to the shore, in order thereto asking for men and a pilot, whom they gave him But the general might only go alone, and they requested four other Portuguese in exchange: the general once more maintained that his people were not Portuguese but Zealanders, but consented that three of his men should remain on land. Thus the general went on board with eleven Cingales, whom having on board, he asked that they would help to remove some casks and packages. For this purpose they came below into the hold, and being there he had the hatch put on, and kept them below. He took the interpreter with other Cingales, and showed them many costly goods and said, "Go ashore with two other Cingales men, and tell the king that I shall keep the eight men until he sends my men on board; tell him also of the goods that you have seen, which are for the king, but he must send pepper and cinnamon." The general also wrote a letter to the king, admonishing him to guard himself from evil counsellors. If he had cinnamon and pepper, we had goods enough to pay him. And the reason why he had kept the eight men on board was, because they had so foolishly requested him to bring the ship and goods on land without their seeing any appearance there of pepper or cinnamon to pay in exchange;[19] also that they considered him and his men as Portuguese, whereby they might easily take occasion, the goods being on land, to confiscate them; and if the king were pleased in future to deal with uprightness, he would willingly give the king satisfaction in everything with all respect and friendship. With this letter the general sent once again some presents, still hoping to get cinnamon and pepper. Moreover the general let all the flags and standards wave and the cannon be fired off all round in honour of the king, which caused him more horror than honour.[20]

The same ditto the king sent a canoe with the interpreter, wherein was very much refreshment, of deer's flesh, fowls butter and other fruits; (and)[21] made offer to the general that he might make use of his country everywhere. Our three men also came back on board, (the king) begging that we would not depart nor change our place, (for) he would expedite our lading; offered us to leave on board always as surety three or four men of his Cingales, apologised for the misunderstanding about bringing the ship and goods on land, and begged that he might be granted time, he was having the pepper gathered: but it was all deceit.

The 7th June the king sent a sample of pepper, which he priced very dear, also some wax; but the general would not offer for so little, nor make any purchase.

The 8th ditto the king departed from the shore, as he saw that his attempt would not succeed.

---

19. The ed. of 1617 omits "in exchange."

20. In orig. "dat hen meer verwaerden als vereerden,"—a play on words.

21. The ed. of 1617 inserts "the king."

The 9th ditto we fetched water and other refreshment from the land, and learnt through others that spoke Portuguese that the king of Matecalo was under tribute to the Portuguese.[22]

The 10th June the general sent two men to the king, (asking) if, considering[23] we gave him time, he could help us to lading. The king promised once more that he knew how to bring it about, but it must be procured from where the great king was, for which purpose he should send some men thitherwards with one of our clerks. The general on hearing this answer resolved to go himself, as he understood that there was another great king of Candy.[24] He requested of the king of Matecalo five persons in hostage, whom the king sent, to wit, one of his councillors Panneka[25] and two other captains, with two other persons besides. So there came again elephants to the shore. The general went to speak to the king of Matecalo, who dissuaded him from going to Candy, as the way was long and difficult, so that it was resolved that a clerk should be sent thitherwards with divers presents.

The 15th ditto the general came on board again, and as one had to bide the time of the return of the clerk sent, every day we bartered for so many precious stones of ruby, balass, topaz, *baccan*,[26] garnets, spinels, jacinths, sapphires white and blue, *olias de guattes*[27] and crystal, so that we got together a fair quantity. The most that it cost us was the presents that one had to give to the king of Matecalo, in order to have leave to trade : the stones are of little value, but we gave little for them.

The 3rd July the clerk returned from the king of Candy with two agents of the same king's, also letters to the general with presents of gold rings, and other great arrows called

---

22. See infra. note 72

23. The ed. of 1617 has "seeing."

24. This betrays strange ignorance on the part of the Dutch regarding Ceylon.

25. Bannekarala, doubtless. (cf. C. A. S. Jl. x. 158 and note). See Bree's narrative.

26. Malay *bakam*, ruby. Evidently the writer obtained this name later on at Achin or Bantam. It is used again (infra.)

27. For *olhos de Gato* (Port), cat-s'eyes.

segonsios.[28] The aforesaid king offered through his letters and agents Gonsael Roderigos and Melchior Rebecca[29] all friendship and lading that he was able (to give), begging that the general would come and visit him in his royal court, Candy.

The same evening arrived Guionlefort with his boat, at which there was great joy, because the ship the *Ram* had now been separated from us since the 24th December near the Capo bon Esperance. Therefore it was unitedly resolved that the general should proceed to the great king, as also because he had such an order from the gentlemen his owners to go and speak with the aforenamed king, presenting letters from his excellency, and the friendship of his friends, and enemy of his enemies.

Thus the general set out the 6th July, taking with him divers presents, and accompanied by the men, among whom were some that played on instruments, the General not shumning the long way and great fatigue.

The *Ram* coming to anchor beside the admiral, some shots were fired in honour of the king's agents, (and) the gunner firing more than he was ordered was wounded by the overloading of a cannon that burst, from which he died.

* * * *

All the time whilst the general was absent we refreshed and provided the ship the *Ram*, meanwhile bartering for some more precious stones. We also sent off the shallop to some other places to seek for a better roadstead, but found none better than here off the *playe*[30] of Matecalo.

The 28th July came the general again on board from the king of Candy, and left behind at two days' journey Captain

---

28. Spelt *sergonsios* further on (sarakunta). The word represents Port. *Zarguncho,* the origin of which I cannot find. In Pyrard ii 378 it is spelt *Ziconti*, and the manufacture is described. The arrow was from the earliest times in Ceylon the symbol of authority (cf. Parker's *Ancient Ceylon* 551, and see plate 5 in Davy's *Ceylon*, where the king is represented holding an arrow like a sceptre).

29. Gonsalo Rodriguez and Melchior Rebello (?), two Portuguese renegades apparently

30. This represents Span. *Playa,* seashore.

Jongerhelt,[31] who through sickness and fatigue could not follow: he left him three elephants and six men to help him over the road, who also arrived the last ditto. Further what befell him (the general) in the journey to Candy, also in the town and court of the king, and in returning, shall here follow.

The general setting out[32] for Candy came to the house of the king of Matecalo,[33] who entertained him splendidly with the agents from Candy, presented the general with gold rings (and) provided elephants, men, *pallenkins*,[34] to carry him and his goods, also any of his people that could not walk; this convoy he furnished as far as into the territory of the old king[35]. Wherever they came they were well entertained without having to pay anything therefor. Coming into the territory of the old king, the *modeliar* met us with pipes and drums, who brought us into an *aldea*,[36] where they were well entertained, and the chamber and sleeping-place behung with white cloths, which is one of the greatest honours that one does there in the country of Celon. The general presented the old king with some presents, as also his *modeliar*, and sent a man to the aforesaid king, who begged that the general in returning would come and visit them, promising him that if he would at another time come to his coast or shore[37] all friendship should befall him.

---

31. Further on described as "of Flushing." He was Captain of musketeers on the *Ram*, and died in Achin on 21st Feb., 1603.

32. On 6th July.

33. Rijcks (infra, D 3), calls it "the king of Battekelce's palace."

34. In ed. of 1617 "pollenkens."

35. As will be seen from the statement further on, a daughter of this "old king" was "one of the wives of the king of Candy:" Both the *Mahavamsa* and the *Rajavaliya* call Dona Cathrina Vimaladharma's "chief queen," but how many sub-queens he had, I do not know. (cf. de Weert's statement infra C 1). His first wife, one of the daughters of Tamvita or Udammita Rala, he repudiated with his Christianity, and she married a Portuguese in Columbo (see *Rajav.* 90, 100. I cannot identify this "old king" or his daughter.

36. Port. for "village." Comparing the itinerary near the end with the statement below that the next *aldea* stopped at was "two miles" from this one, this village should be "Neguritty," a name which I think is certainly meant for Nikawetiya, which village is a little within the boundary of Uva. ("Neguritti" is probably a misreading for "Nequuitti.")

37. Over what "coast or shore" this man exercised authority is not clear.

The general proceeding further was carried with men, goods and *pallinckens* as far as the *aldea* of a queen, being two miles from there.[38] This queen is the daughter of the aforesaid old king, and now one of the wives of the king of Candy, who had given her this *aldea* ; but she had left for Vintane, where we arrived the next day.[39] Near the town of Vintane there came to meet us some six *modeliars* accompanied by much people, pipes, drums, horns and other instruments, in honour of the general, and brought him into the town of Vintane, where he was brought into his lodging, which was also behung with white cloth.[40] And we stayed there two nights. There was the aforesaid queen, who caused the general to be informed that she desired to see him, and urged that if he journeyed back again through her territory, he should ask for all that he had need of.

This town of Vintane[41] is situated on the river of Trinquamale, where are made fine galleys and *champanes* for the service of the king of Candy; it is situated nine miles from the sea, and by land from Matecalo one-and-twenty miles Singales, which is about two German miles, and nine

---

38. This must be the "Nilvaele" of the itinerary, which name evidently represents Nilgala, a village about seven miles from Nika-wetiya. Here the Danish Admiral Ove Giedde spent a night in August 1621, on his return from Bintenne. It was here that, in September 1640, the Dutch Admiral Coster was murdered by the Kandyans (see *C. Lit. Reg.* ii, 350).

39. According to the itinerary "Vintane" is 6 miles from, "Vegamme" (Bibile Wegama), which is 4 miles from "Nilvaele." In English miles the distances are Nilgale to Bibile 14, Bibile to Alutnuwara (Bintenna) 20 to 30, according to route.

40. Ove Giedde was accorded the same kind of reception in August 1621 on his arrival at "Venthanen."

41. On Bintenne or Alutnuwara see White's *Manual of Uva* Chap. iii.

miles from Candy.[42] In the town of Vintane is a great *pagode*: the base is in circumference a hundred and thirty paces (it is) very handsome and high, all white and gilt above, in the manner of a pyramid, but from below ascending ovalwise up to a four-cornered point. And there are yet other *pagodes* besides, also a monastery wherein are monks clad in yellow clothes, and they go along the streets with large *sombareros*;[43] some have slaves with them who carry the *sombareros* and serve them. They are clean shaven after the manner of the monks in this country, only that one sees no corona. They also go with paterrosters[44] in their hands, continually[45] babbling or reading. They are held in great honour, and are free from working and all other burdens. Their monastery is after the manner of our monasteries in this country, with their galleries, corridors and many private chapels which are gilt, wherein stand many figures of men and women, who they say lived holily. These carved figures stand adorned with silvern gilt clothes; they are honored day and night with lamps, and wax candles; they stand on altars where are large chandeliers, which are held by carved naked children. Into the aforesaid chapels come the monks at all hours to read their prayers and breviaries. While there they[46]

---

42. In the itinerary the distance by road from Matecalo to Vintane comes to 21½ miles, these being Sinhalese miles according to statement here, each of which the writer says (or means to say), equals two German miles. Reckoning the German mile at about four English miles, this would make the total distance 162 miles, English. which is very incorrect, the actual distance from Sammanturai to Alutnuwara via Nilgala by the present road being about 70 miles. The distance of Bintenne from the sea, as here given, is also wrong, the actual distance in a direct line being some 60 miles, The figure given for the distance between Bintenne and Kandy (9 miles) accords with the itinerary, and should equal 18 German miles, that is, about 70 English. From the mention of "Vendro" in the itinerary, it would seem that the course taken from Bintenne was along the present Teldeniya road as far as Galmaloya, thence down to Wenduruwa, up again to join the Teldeniya road, and so to Kandy, —a very roundabout route.—As regards the extraordinary creation of a ghost place "Sigales" owing to a misprint and misunderstanding, see *C. Lit. Reg.* vi, 318 n.s.

43. Umbrellas (see *Hobson-Jobson* s. 5. Sombrero").

44. Rosaries.

45. The ed. of 1617 omits this word.

46. The ed. of 1617 has "I."

saw them holding their festival and saw their procession going along the town. The chief abbot or priest sits upon an elephant clad in silver-and gold, and the abbot holds a golden staff above his head fast with both his hands. Before him go in order other monks with much playing of horns, trumpets cymbals, clanging of bells and basins, which altogether gives a very good harmony. Many lamps and torches are also carried, and there follow many men, women and maidens. The most beautiful maidens, ere the procession goes out and comes in again, perform many wondrous feats with dancing; they are all with naked bodies bare above, the arms, hands and ears half adorned with gold and precious stones ; below they have handsome embroidered clothes. These people one sees daily before the *pagodes* and in the chapels doing *sombayo*,[47] which is, to fall flat down on the earth, (then) standing up holding the hands together over the head, and so saying their prayers. Anyone observing these things of the monks, monasteries and processions would certainly judge that our monks had learnt most of their ceremonies from these heathens. They also have the custom of presenting flowers to their idols, which stand everywhere on the roads, some near trees, and others in built niches, as the Jesuits now[48] put the image of Mary everywhere.

Departing from the town of Vintane we came to the *aldea*[49] of the king's son, where all good entertainment was given to us. Being a day's journey from Candy, the king sent his own *pallenkin* with certain elephants, when the general let the other *pallenkin* and the other people from Vintane return. This *pallenkin* of the king's was nobly equipped with gilded coverings; and at all hours he sent people with victuals, fruits and wine, which he has had planted in Candy itself, and it is very good strong wine, as if it were grown in

---

47. See infra, F 5, note 5.
48. The ed. of 1617 omits these two words.
49. From the itinerary it is to be inferred that this was Wendaruwa (see Laurie's *Gaz. C. P.*, which, however, says nothing of any connection with royalty.)

Portugal.[50] Near the town of Candy coming to a river, the general had to stop there. and he was accompanied by many gentlemen *modeliers*, who are captains. Having stopped there an hour, the king sent his chief *modelier*, Emanuel Dics,[51] with many other Portuguese, all of whom had their ears slit[52] serving the aforesaid king. There our general was received and was thus accompanied to the town of Candy by some thousand armed soldiers of all nations, such as Turks, Moors, Singales, Cafferos and renegade Portuguese. He had by him eight flags flying, among which were some that they had recently taken from the Portuguese.[53] In the reception there was much noise of all kinds of strange instruments among all there were shawns and sackbuts;[54] which played several pieces of music in good time. And thus was our general conducted to his lodging past the palace of the king, where they made a great demonstration with firing. Our general was accompanied by Captain Jongerhelt of Flushing, three trumpetors before him, and one that bore the bannerol or prince's flag ; he had also with him four other attendants. There was also carried a silk Spanish or Portuguese[55] flag all trailing, which was presented to the king, in return for which the king gave another Portuguese flag that he had captured from the Portuguese. Having come into the lodging, all was arranged and put in order, not in the Singales but in the Portuguese fashion and Emanuel Dios with other Portuguese remained to keep the general company.

---

50. That this was *grape* wine, the produce of vines planted by Vimaladharma, is proved by the statement of de Weert, infra, C 1, note 79. (The footnote on this subject in C. *L. I. Reg.* vi, 325, needs emendation).

51. Manual Dias, a renegade Portuguese, captured at the great defeat of the army of Pedro Lopes de Sousa in 1594 (see infra.)

52. Lit. "cut up" (opghesneden). On the boring of renegades' ears see C. A. S. Jl. xx, 339 n. 4). Tennent (*Ceylon* ii, 35) speaks of "Portuguese prisoners, many of them deprived of their ears," which is one of his blunders.

53. See infra.

54. The ed. of 1617 alters "sackebouten" to "sackpijpen" (bagpipes).

55. Spain and Portugal were then invited. With characteristic inaccuracy Tennent (ii 35) describes this incident thus :—" Spilberg, besides the banner of the United Provinces, caused a standard-bearer to lay at the feet of the king the flag of Portugal *with the blazon reversed* (*Italics* in orig.)."

In the afternoon the king sent three horses equipped with their saddles, and begged the general to come to him. Accordingly he went to the king, taking with him some presents. After the king had received him, the presents were laid upon a carpet the king clothed in white stood up and showing the aforesaid presents to his young prince and princess,[56] began to walk along the hall with the general. Having had some conversation with one another, the king gave the general his permission to go to his lodging. He said: "Tomorrow we shall speak again. Go and rest a bit: I know that you are tired with travelling." Ere the general departed he made his musicians play, to the great pleasure of the king. On his departure all the shawms, trumpets and sackbuts[57] played.

The next day the king of Candy again sent the general his horses and had him come to court, where he was again received ceremoniously. The king speaking with him of the business regarding cinnamon and pepper, the general was not willing to agree to the price that the king demanded, so they let the talk of business drop, and came to other discourses. The general wishing to take leave of the king, the king asked him what he would give therefor. The general answered that he had not come there for pepper or cinnamon, but simply to obey the command of his excellency, which was to offer the king friendship on behalf of his princely excellency, and if he had need of assistance, that his princely excellency would send it him against the Portuguese his enemies. The king listening to this repeated it to his lords, who received it thankfully with great satisfaction. The king took the general in his arm and lifted him up,[58] saying: "All the pepper and cinnamon that I have ready is given to you;"—which was little, and might be worth here in Holland about three thousand pounds Flemish, making the excuse that we had come upon him suddenly as if fallen from heaven, so that he had no cinnamon or pepper ready, since he had never in his life traded in it, and also no one might gather the

56. See infra.
57. The ed. of 1617 has "bagpipes."
58. *cf.* de Weert's statement, infra, C. I.

cinnamon, yea he even caused it to be destroyed on account of his enemies the Portuguese, that these should not come and get it; and for us to stay there longer was impossible, on account of the heavy rain, which was the reason that no cinnamon could be obtained, also that the *mosson* from the east was beginning, whereby we lay upon a lee shore at Matecalo.

Between the king and our general there were many conversations every day. The king showed the general all the arms that they had captured from the Portuguese, which were cuirasses, morions and others, also all his *pagodes*, which are many and costly, and which have more than four or five thousand carved figures, some as high as masts, for which special towers are made very costly and cleverly wrought of beautiful stone, all vaulted and gilt; and indeed their *pagodes* far surpass the Popish churches in handsome building. After the general had seen all this he returned to the king who asked him what he thought of the *pagodes*. He answered that he had rather see living personages than dead figures which could do no service at all. The king asked him if our *pagodes* were like the Portuguese adorned with images, naming Maria, Petro, Paulo, and others, and if we also believed in Christ. The general answered that we were Christians like the Portuguese. He also wished to be informed of what we had in our churches. We showed him the bare wall, but said that we had in our hearts the true God who had created heaven and earth and all of us. The king asked once more if our God could not die, whereupon admirable proof was given him that no mortal man could be divine and we said to him openly that his figures were in vain, as in all cases they are of dead persons. He was also openly admonished that he should not rely upon his *pagodes* but upon God who had created all; which the king well understood, and pointed to his palace and city, saying: "All this had God given me." He deplored that his Singales were so greedy, without conscience, that they steal and take all that they can conceal. Thereupon the general answered that we could conceal nothing, but God could see it in heaven, and what he did not punish here would not remain unpunished hereafter. The king understanding this well made a fine speech, and said: "It is true, for such as one sows one shall reap."[59] Other conversations took place too long to be given here.

The next day the king again sent the horses and had the general come to his court as guest with all his people into a large hall that was hung all round with tapestry, where were placed many Spanish chairs and a table on which all was prepared in the manner of Christians, and enlivened with much music and other playing. The general presented the king with the portrait of his princely excellency sitting on horseback in full armour in form and si e of horse and person, as he appeared at the battle in Flanders *A.D.* 1600 on 2 July,[60] with which the king was wonderfully pleased. The plan of this battle was described to him, and also the position of our United Netherlands, and how the States General under the direction of his princely excellency carried on the war against the king of Portugal and Castille.

The general was for five days most of the time with the king. The king was never tired of asking about the condition, position and nature of our lands. The king had the portrait of his excellency hung in his room that it might always be in his sight. The general was brought into the chamber of the queen, where she sat with her children the prince and princess, all clad in the manner of Christians,[61] the king showing the general the aforesaid personages, which is a great honour and favour. The king said: "See, I, my queen, prince and princess will help to carry on their shoulders the stones, lime and other things, if the states and his princely excellency be pleased to come and make a castle here in my country: they should be allowed to choose for that purpose such place, harbour, or bay, as they shall find suitable." To this end the king gave our general divers letters, and made him his ambassador to negotiate the matters that might be concluded with the States General and his excellency. His

59. The good Calvinist diarist did not realise that the king was simply enunciating the Buddhist doctrine of *karma*.

60. When Prince Maurice defeated the Archduke Albert near Nieuwpoort. The ed. of 1617 has "1602" for "1600.")

61. Dona Catharina never abjured Christianity, as Vimaladharma had done (cf. infra.)

royal majesty of Candy also honoured our general with presents[62] and titles. The king asked the general for some of his instruments of music, which he liberally presented to the king, with two persons who could play very well on all instruments, which the king took with such gratitude that it seemed as if no greater friendship could be shown him. These two persons are master Hans Rempell and Erasmus Matsberger.[63] These aforesaid persons the king took into his court, and himself began to learn to play on several instruments. Moreover the prince and princess made Erasmus Matsberger their secretary.[64] The king with his prince and princess began to learn to speak the Netherlands language, saying: "Candy is now Flanders." So that the king showed himself delighted with everything, and our general was very welcome, who had instructed him well in everything, so that we do not doubt that he will be a great friend to us, and become a greater enemy to the Portuguese.[65]

The general departed from Candy,[66] taking his adieu of his royal majesty named in the Singales language Fimala Derma Suri Ada. (The meaning of these names will be given in another place in the history of Celon, of what has occurred since the death of the great king Darma.[67]) To our general were furnished many elephants and men in order to return to his ships, also giving him large arrows called *sergonios*,

62. Among these was the large pyrope, of which the first edition of the journal gives an exact representation, calling it a "carbuncle or ruby."

63. In a previous part of this journal, the writer, describing the doings of the Dutch at "Mulaly" (Mohilla, one of the Comoro Islands), says:—"The 27 ditto (Feb. 1602) the general again sent the captain of the country some presents with master Hans Trumpeter and Erasamus Matsbergher, who let him hear music on divers instruments, in which he took great pleasure."

64. See infra; D 2, at note 49. Tennent (ii 36) says:—"The admiral at the request of the king, left behind him his secretary (sic), with two musicians of his band."

65. The writer little realized how soon the friendly relations would be destroyed.

66. No dates are given from the day Spilbergen left Matecalo (6th July) to the day of his return (28th July). Allowing six days for the journey each way, the Dutch general appears to have spent nine or ten days in the royal town.

67. See infra, where no explanation is given of the names. "Ada" appears to be a corruption of *adghasim*, royal highness.

wishing thereby to corroborate their great trust and sincerity,[68] also a gilt *somberero*. with four or five slaves to serve him. Thus the general returned through the whole country free and easy without any cost, except only some presents that he gave voluntarily. And he was (absent) on this expedition two-and-twenty days.

The general having come on board began to make preparations for the ships to depart towards *ultimo* August, as then was to be expected the *mosson* from the east. Finding himself weak in men (only two-and-twenty souls),[69] he gave orders to transfer some of the crew of the *Ram*, which had still five-and-forty men, against which some disrespectfully set themselves, but the general knew so well how to check that, that equally well he effected his purpose, and with weighty reasons persuaded the others and overcame their rash plump disobedience, so as to make their conscience and even judgment cause them to stand ashamed and convinced whenever anything is said on the subject.[70] The general put all these questions on one side, and did what was needful for the success of our voyage.

The 5th August there followed from Candy the *modeliar* or great captain Emanuel Dios, accompanied by other *modeliars* and one hundred-and-twenty soldiers, who was sent by the king to view the ships and to speak with the general about looking for some suitable place for the ships to anchor in at other times. Thereupon many discussions and written promises took place between them, which were sworn to in evidence of their trust. The aforenamed *modeliar* was also shown all honour and brought on board by two shallops of armed men, whereat he was greatly gratified.

The 8th August we saw a sail to seaward. The general had his shallop manned, which captured the sail, and found her to be a galliot of about forty lasts, new and well built, whereon were six-and-forty men, both Portuguese, *Toupases*,

---

68. See supra note 28.
69. Lit. "eaters."
70. From a later entry we learn that Guion Lefort, the vice-admiral on the *Ram* was deposed on account of being suspected of complicity in a conspiracy and mutiny, doubtless that here spoken of.

Mesticos and *Marineros*, who had some spingards and two bases, with many pikes and partisans, but allowed her to be captured by the general's shallop, in which were fourteen men. The captain of the galliot was named Antonio de Costa Montero. She was laden with *arrecca*, of little value to us, and contained some pepper and cinnamon. The *modeliar* Emanuel Dios seeing that was fully convinced that we were enemies of the Portuguese, and some of the weapons were presented to him, and the galliot with the cargo was presented to the king, regarding which a man was sent expressly to Candy to convey the news thither. The king caused great rejoicings to be made.

The 9th ditto the aforesaid *modeliar* departed, and there went with him once more Guion Lefort and Hertoch Philip in order to further the despatch of the promised cinnamon and pepper, which arrived very shortly after their departure, —60 canasters of cinnamon, 16 bales of pepper, 4 bales of turmeric. Guion Lefort coming to Candy with his company was also well received, and received some gold rings as a present, as also Hertoch Philips. There was more cinnamon there but the road, which is long, takes much time, so that we could not stay there longer on account of the *mosson*. During the time that Guion Lefort was away the ships were provided and cleared.

The 11th ditto we again captured a champaigne[71] with *arrecca*, which was presented with the cargo to the king of Matecalo, who had formerly given the general leave to capture the Portuguese, and had to that end given assistance, but now made protests that they captured the Portuguese off his territory: but he must have done this out of dissimulation, as he is neutral in regard to contribution.[72]

The 12th ditto we saw to seaward another *champaigne*, which we went to and brought into the roadstead (it was also laden with *arrecca*), upon which were twenty men, *mesticos* and *toupas*. The *arrecca* we sold daily in exchange for precious stones and refreshments.

---

71. A small vessel (see *Hobson-Jobson s.v.*(Sampan).)
72. cf. Supra, note 22.

Meanwhile Antonio de Costa Montero escaped from us through bad watching, for which the person of Claes Cales and others were punished. It appeared that some Portuguese wished to ransom the ships; but it was more to detain us, so that the *mosson* should surprise us. In these three ships were about a hundred men, of whom some stayed to serve us, and a part were sent to Candy; the rest were pitched overboard, and escaped by swimming ashore.

The 23rd August an accident took place once again on the *Ram*, to the gunner Houtepen, through careless handling, in that while firing a piece and reloading it he did not wipe it out well, so that he lost his life.

The 1st September Guion Lefort with his company came on board from Candy, who brought letters from the king with some presents; and as the *mosson* was at hand we resolved to depart the next day, seeing that the Portuguese were only attempting deceit in order to have the *mosson* fall upon us, and so to have a lee shore, whereby we should have run great danger: therefore we left at night between the Monday and Tuesday. The general first went on land on the *play* of Matecalo, where were some two hundred Singales who sold all kinds of wares, asking them if he was indebted to anyone, if they had any demand to make that they should speak, his shallops were there with goods for payment, but each said to him that they had nothing to demand. So we set sail in the night of the 2nd ditto, setting fire to two Portuguese ships laden with *arrecca*: we had no time to sell the *arrecca*, and we also wished thereby to show the Singales that we are enemies of the Portuguese.

Thus, God be praised, we departed from the island of Celon, where our general had run no small peril, both with the king of Matecalo, who is a contributory of the Portuguese, as also in the journey to Candy; the far road and the great fatigue; but all was done in order to follow out the orders of the owners and in hope of our lading. When leaving the land two men ran away, who were the gunner and the carpenter of the admiral.[73]

---

73. See infra, C 1. note 6.

Thus in God's name we departed the 3rd September for Achien in the island of Sumatra.

B. 2- SHORT ACCOUNT OR HISTORY OF WHAT HAS HAPPENED IN THE ISLAND OF CELON SINCE THE DEATH OF THE KING RAGU, AND HOW THE KINGDOM OF CANDY SITUATED IN THE ISLAND OF CELON FREED ITSELF FROM THE PORTUGUESE RULE.[74]

The king in Celon named Mara Ragu[75] had three sons, lawful heirs and a bastard son named Darma, who was born in Setavacca, where the kings hold their court in Selon. This bastard Darma was got by a *bailliarderse*,[76] who are women that the king maintains for their good and skilful dancing. This Darma was educated in warfare, conducting himself bravely and wisely, so that he managed to draw the hearts of the soldiers to himself, whereby he was emboldened to proceed to an evil deed, killing and murdering his father Mara Ragu and his three brothers the lawful heirs, when having the power in his hands he came into the town of Settavacca, and there caused himself to be received and acknowledged as king of Celon, exercising great tyranny over the Singales, who bore no good feeling towards him on account of the wicked deed before mentioned. That he was no barber's son as some write, we inquired into carefully, but a son of Mara Ragu as above related.[77] It may well be that he was an amateur of the surgeon's art, as he was a brave soldier and a lover of much knowledge. He made great warfare on the Portuguese, so that he captured all their forts (and) *trancqueros*[78] except Coulombo and Mannar.[79]

74. The facts here recorded appear to have been collected during the stay of the Dutch in Ceylon (cf. infra).

75. This appears to be a corruption of "Maha Rajju (ruwo)." The person meant is Mayadunne.

76. A Corrupt form of Port. *bailadeira*, dancers.

77. On the above see C. A. S. Jl. xx. 271 n. 5, 272, n. 1.

78. Stockades (Port. tranqueira).

79. Regarding the warfare waged by Raja Sinha I. (here curiously called "Darma," through some confusion, apparently, with Dharmapala) against the Portuguese, see C. A. S. Jl. xx. 173-395.

In this aforesaid island of Celon is another kingdom named Candy, which never became subject or submissive to the kings that hold their court in Setavacca. The kingdom of Candy is very powerful, rich in inhabitants mostly Singales, who would never acknowledge the aforesaid Darma as king, but waged war with him, and were assisted by the Portuguese.

The Singhales ever hating the aforesaid Darma for his tyranny so brought about matters that he died of poison[80]. These Singales, who are the greatest proportion of the inhabitants, straightway[81] made terms with the Portuguese, and so remain in peace without giving any, or little, tribute to the Portuguese ; so that the death of the king Darma formed a great entrance and road for the Portuguese in Celon, who since make fortresses everywhere in all harbours, bays and places according to their good pleasure. They let the Singales freely use their heathen ceremonies and *pagodes* : yea, many Portuguese unite and marry with the Singales, so that they have an *olypoderigo*[82] among each other ; from which it appears that the Portuguese their affection tends more towards riches than towards the Romish faith or religion. The Portuguese live much amongst the heathenish Singales, in divers places where they have no church, hermitage, chapel, nor monks, priest, or sacristan, being like the inhabitants in many things.

At the same time there happened to die the king of Candy,[83] where at that time the great *modeliar* was Fimala Derma Suri Ada. The aforenamed Fimala Derma Suri Ada had in his youth been brought from Candy to Coulombo. He was the son of a great prince in Candy who was also great *modeliar*. This aforenamed Fimala was baptised in Coulombo and given the name of the brother of King Philip of Spain and Portugal, Don Joan Daustria.[84] From Coulombo he was taken to Goa, and was there at the time that Emanuel Sosa Cottin[85] was governor in Goa, and also (when) Mattheo

80. This does not accord with the statements of other authorities (see C. A. S. Jl. xx. 395.)

81. By an oversight, the ed. of 1617 here omits a couple of lines

82. *Olla podrida* (Spain), hotchpotch.

83. Dom Filippe (see C. A. S. Jl. xx. 391).

84. For the history of Dom Joao de Austria and the events hereafter recorded, see C. A. S. Jl. xx. 294. n. 5, 389 et. seq.

85. Manual de Sousa Coutinho (1588-91).

Alberckt[86] came from Portugal as viceroy. And so this Fimala Derma Suri Ada was baptised a Christian, became big and strong, was very sturdy on his legs, and a man of great strength and clever of wit. He was made by the Portuguese, as before said, great *modeliar* or captain in Candy, this great *modeliar* being the next person to the king, who had much authority and conducted the carrying on of war.

The king of Candy being dead, (and) this Don Ian, who had the soldiers in his interest, and was also loved by the Singales, as he was likewise a Singales, of noble birth and house in Candy, made himself king, and smote dead and expelled all the Portuguese who were in Candy and dwelt there freely, setting himself in open warfare against the Portuguese. There was in Candy a lawful heir, a daughter of the aforesaid deceased king's, who was taken by the Portuguese to Mannar, and baptized by the name of Dona Catharina. The Portuguese came with a great force from Goa and other places, under the command of Petro Lopes de Sosa,[87] general and captain of Mallacca, to Candy, bringing with them Dona Catharina, daughter of the deceased king, and lawful heir of Candy, in order to place her on the throne by force. And the aforenamed Lopes de Sosa was to marry this Dona Catharina when she was established in her kingdom, and he was to have the rule there in Candy, as married to the queen.

So the aforenamed Lopes betook himself with his force to Candy, causing Don Ian to retreat, who was then in Candy. Don Ian betook himself into the *watto*[88] and woods, where he cut off supplies from the general Lopes ; and all Portuguese that ventured on the roads or outside of Candy were smitten dead, so that the general Lopes was forced to withdraw to a mile from Candy, to a place named Ballene, in order to give battle to Don Ioan Daustria, otherwise in Singales style named

86. Mathias de Albuquerque (1591-97).
87. Pedro Lopes de Sousa.
88. Port. *Mato*, Jungle.

Fimala Derma Suria. Thus these aforesaid personages *Anno* 1590[89] on a Sunday each with his force fell very fiercely upon the other; for the general Lopes was well provided with good soldiers, and Don Ian likewise with many of his inhabitants. The Portuguese had forty big elephants that were accustomed to war; but Don Joan fell upon them in such wise, continuing to fight with pikes, *flesios*,[90] *sergonsios*[91] and other weapons, that the Portuguese had no time to rest; they were also so beset that they could obtain no food. The aforenamed Don Ioan separated the Portuguese from each other, and they were altogether defeated. Petro Lopes de Sosa was left there dead, Dona Catharina prisoner, all the elephants captured, and many Portuguese made slaves. By this victory Don Ioan then established himself firmly as king in Candy and married Dona Catharina himself, by whom he had the present prince and princess.[92] Dona Catharina was at that time between 9 and 10 years old.[93]

The cause of this victory cannot be ascribed, judging in human fashion, to the strength of the Singales: it was, next to God who holds all armies in his hand, the skilful conduct of Don Ioan, who again had most of his soldiers of foreign nations, because the Singales are indeed fine men but love great ease, people that like to eat good food and to do little work. They are also people that are almost universally well off in goods, houses and other things, priding themselves much of their *Castes* and consider it a great disgrace to do any work. And they eat alone, have their food served on *bonnannes*[94] leaves, always drink out of *gorgelanes*,[95] that is, out of a pot with a spout without putting their mouth thereto;[96] and whatever they have touched and have not eaten they throw away for the dogs: no slaves so wretched as to be willing to eat such as has once been touched.

---

89. An error for 1594.
90. Arrows (Port. *Flecha* or *frecha*).
91. See supra, note 28.
92. See infra, C 1.
93. De Weert (infra, C 1), on the authority of Vimaladharma himself, says she was twelve.
94. Banana, Plantain (cf infra.)
95. See *Hobson-Jobson* s.5. "Goglet."
96. See the picture and description in Knox's *Hist. Rel.* 87.

After the Portuguese had had this defeat, Don Ioan Daustria, now king of Candy, had his kingdom free, and destroyed all the *tranqueros* of the Portuguese, as they had almost all been smitten dead, captured and fled to Coulombo. So that now Don Ioan having peace had a very costly palace built in Candy, and also many towers and *pagodes*, at which all the Portuguese that had been captured had to work and he caused all his buildings to be made in the Christian style. The aforenamed Don Ioan also had his court fortified with ramparts,[97] and (had) divers *tranqueros* (made) in certain suitable places, where he constantly holds a good and strong garrison, well mounted, so that they can hardly reach Candy, to wit, his foes, the Portuguese. He is always occupied with buildings and in trying novelties in order to withstand his enemies. He captured in the defeat of the general Lopes some hundred *banderos*.[98] He presented our general with many weapons of all kinds that he had captured in his victory.

Three or four years after the defeat of the general Lopes, Dom Jeronimo des Ovedo, [99] general of the conquest in Celon, made many attempts and efforts to conquer the kingdom of Candy, but was not able to effect anything of importance, until at last he came with a great force by command of the king of Spain and Portugal, bringing with him many *cavallieros fidalgos*[100] from Goa, of whom there are whole dozens in number, intending to swallow up Candy at once. He came to the aforesaid place of Ballene, where formerly the battle with the general Lopes took place, where Dom Ioan king of Candy met him, and there they gave battle to each other, which was very fierce and also lasted long; and but that Dom Jeronimo kept himself with his men so firmly serried, they would all have been slain like the general Lopes; but he managed to keep his force in order, retreating and fighting, although he was pursued and driven back as far as Coulombo. It was reckoned to the great honour of

97. See *Mahan* xciv.
98. Port. *Bandeira*, flag
99. Dom Jeronimo de Azevedo.
100. The ed. of 1617 has "hidalgos" (the Spanish form).

the aforenamed Jeronimo that he brought himself and most of his men *in salvo* in such order while fighting for five days; although indeed many Portuguese fell in the fighting, as well as of the king's troops.[101] Since that time the Portuguese have made no further attempt with any forces against the king of Candy, but daily make skirmishes from their *tranqueros* and some excursions. The *tranqueros* both of the king and of the Portuguese lie at a mile and some at half a mile from each other. Frequently by surprises and ruses, and also by bribing with money, which also succeeds there, they have now and then captured a *tranquerin*[102] from each other.

About eight months ago, on Easter day *Anno* 1602,[103] Emanuel Dios, now great *modeliar* in Candy, who was a youth at the time of the general Lopes, and having been taken prisoner by the king remained in Candy to serve, returned once more to the Portuguese in Coulombo, to Don Jeronimo des Ovedo, and suggested many plans for killing the king of Candy, who was very welcome, and was much trusted, and also let his ears be clipped, since all the Portuguese that serve in Candy must also have their ears adorned in the manner of the Singales[104]. This aforesaid Emanuel Dios set to work to carry out his double dealing. Having agreed with Don Jeronimo, and a silver cross having been brought before him, he was sworn thereby that he should go with five other Portuguese, namely Christaen Jacobino, Albert Primero, Ian Pererro,[105] being all three captains,

---

101. This is not the *famosa retirada* (famous retreat), which took place in 1603. It may be the engagement recorded by Conto in Dec. XII v. i (see C. A. S. Jl. xx. 441-4), which took place in 1599-1600.

102. This appears to represent the Port. diminutive form *tranqueirinha*. It is used again below.

103. As Easter day in 1602 fell on 2 April (O.S.), this must have been written at Achin in December. The events here described are not recorded by any Portuguese writer, as far as I know. It will be seen that the information was obtained from the king himself.

104. This is a very confused statement: the writer, of course, does not mean that Manual Dias had his ears clipped by the Portuguese he is but repeating what he told us above.

105. Apparently Christovao Jacome (?), Alberto Pinhiero, and Joao Pereira.

with two other soldiers to Candy, betaking themselves to the king in order to serve him, and so to find occasion to murder the king. This aforesaid Emanuel Dios succeeded in persuading Don Jeronimo of further opportunities of easily murdering the king, for which purpose he received a large sum of money in order to execute the deed and to buy over others to his side to help in that deed. The aforenamed Dios was promised that if he should accomplish his task he should become king in Candy: in default of nothing great promises, for the Portuguese held for certain that if the king were dead they would easily get to the kingdom of Candy. This Don Jeronimo thought that the affair would without doubt have its issue, since it was so confirmed and sworn to on the silver cross. (How Christianly they live in Goa, and everywhere in the East Indies, has been described enough by others: how many murders take place there every night through private quarrels and lusts.)[106].

This Emanuel Dios departed first as if he had escaped from Coulombo, came to Candy to the king, and related all that he had arranged with Don Jeronimo. Don Jeronimo had secretly stationed many Portuguese and other soldiers near the *tranquerin* of Ballene,[107] in order straightway to attack the latter as soon as the deed was accomplished, to wit, when the king was murdered. They imagined that the aforesaid Dios had gone to notify the king that the aforesaid five Portuguese wished to come and serve him with fidelity, and that the king would send orders to his *tranquerin* to receive them when they came over: but other orders were sent there. The king caused the fort of Ballene to be filled with soldiers by night, and himself went into the fort. The aforesaid five Portuguese arrived, having with them five *transchados*[108], which are knives from Iappan, were taken in by Emanuel Dios, and when they came inside

---

106. The reference is evidently to chap. 92 of Linschoten's *Voyagie*.

107. This was the Sinhalese fort. A few years later D. Jeronymo de Azevedo built and garrisoned a stone fortress at Balane (see Boc. 45).

108. Port. *tercado* (older form *trecaao*), a short broad, curved sword.

were led through several chambers to where the king was, and were straightway seized and bound. These Portuguese had some Singales who served them, who seeing that, one of them escaped through the *trancqueros*, notifying this to the Portuguese that lay in ambush. But for the escape of this Singales, the king would have surprised all that lay in ambush. These and such like ruses they practise on both sides, wherefore the Portuguese have a saying "*Esto pretto de Candy sabo mouto*"[109] they mean thereby the king. These five Portuguese remain in Candy rigidly imprisoned. The king relating all this to our general presented him with one of their Iappanese *transchados* with which they intended to kill the king. For this faithful service that Emanuel Dios performed and others besides (because he is a brave soldier of great intelligence and skill), in place of being king as Don Jeronimo had promised him, the king made him his great *modeliar*, which is a high office.

In June last while we were in Celon the aforesaid Emanuel Dios traversed the *matto* with a body of soldiers, and surprised a *tranquerin* wherein was stationed a captain named Simon Corero, smiting dead most of the soldiers, and brought great booty to Candy. [110]

This king of Candy has a fairly large territory, with many towns well built and a pretty good number of people, who are all well-to-do folk, respectable as to their clothes, to wit, as far as the middle of the body, and a *Carpous*[111] on the head. Some that are of large means wear *roppilios*[112] and doublets, much behung with rings in their ears adorned with precious stones, and fine creeses at their

---

109. Correctly, "Este preto de Candia sabe muito," meaning literally, "This black (man) of Kandy knows much," or freely, "This nigger of Kandy knows a thing or two." As regards Vimaladharma's blackness, see infra, C 1.

110. Regarding Simao Correa (who was a Sinhalese) see C. A. S. Jl. xx. 417. n. 1. I have found no other reference to the affair here described.

111. Port. *carapuca*, a kind of cap.

112. Apparently for *roupilha*, dim. of *roupa* (Port), any loose garment.

sides. [113] Their women in like manner go with their breasts bare, being very shamefast when they meet men. Their clothes are neat, and they themselves well fashioned in form and feature; their head dress consists of their own hair, without any fillet of silk or anything else: they manage to fasten it behind the head in such manner as if they wore coifs; their hair lies smoothed back very neatly. In this fashion go all the Singales, great and small. Round their neck, they have silver and gilt necklaces, and rings on their fingers and toes, also round their arms, adorned with precious stones. Their houses are handsome and well built. The women know well how to prepare the food. They live lazily and daintily. They have a country abundant in fowls, fish, deer, peacocks, pigs, butter, milk, and honey; all kinds of fruits, *annanasses* [114]. *bonnanes, coques, jaques, manges,* oranges, lemons and other very good fruit; but no oxen, cows, or buffaloes may they eat, [115] nor drink any wine. Among these Singales dwell many Moors, Turks and other heathens, who have all different laws. The *bramos* [116] are there in great number, who are very superstitious; they are held in honour by other nations. these *bramos* eat nothing that has had life, they also worship any such animals as they see first in the morning (as one may read in Ian Huyghen [117]). Our general asking them why they had this law, they answered that their god had commanded it. Proceeding to further discussions, we said that to our god belonged all that is upon the earth and in the water; and because we are big people and belong to him, he also gives us everything to eat freely, to which they gave no answer. The custom in Celon, Candy and everywhere in the island is, that a man marries as many wives as he is able to maintain. The young girls are hardly

---

113. cf. infra. C I. . The crease appears to have been introduced into Ceylon at an early period, if we are to accept the first quotation in *Hobson-Jobson* s, 5. "Crease" as referring to this weapon. (see also H. Parker's *Ancient Ceylon*. 532) In Baldaeus, *Ceylon* chap. iv. the English translator has twice wrongly rendered *krits* by "Seymetar."

114. Pineapples.

115. Cf. the statements of Bree and Rijcks infra.

116. Brahmans. Buddhist monks are apparently meant.

117. See Linschoten's Voyage (Hak. soc. ed.), i. 224, 248.

ten years old, when they are wedded and bedded[118] They have also the custom of burning their dead. The country is very rich in rice, which is exported to other places; because on the sea-shore in all convenient harbours trade is carried on and there come there large canoes and *champanes*, but all must trade with letters of licence from Portuguese[119], for which they give little. For their safety they submit to give the Portuguese tribute; but if they wished, the Portuguese would be able to do little or nothing; so that the Portuguese are contented with little. The king of Matecalo, who has much territory and people, pays us tribute, and that his people may sail the sea and coast freely, the value of about 50 ducats a year, which he yet pays in rice.

The King of Candy is the only one that wages war without paying tribute, with two brothers, who were also formerly with the Portuguese, and baptized in Coulombo. These help the King of Candy: they are named Don Emanuel and Don Louwis, prince of Set Corle[120]. Other kings may indeed assist the King of Candy, but it takes place secretly. The King of Candy has his territory mostly on both sides of the river of Trinquanemale [121], which river runs past Vintane, a town where the King builds his galleys and *champaines*[122].

The aforesaid island is very rich in cinnamon, and (suitable) for growing pepper, but the Singales have no fancy for it. Only near Coulombo where the Portuguese are is cinnamon gathered. In the Kingdom of Candy is every kind of metal, of iron and copper that is dug there, but little in Matecalo. In Candy are also mountains that yield gold and silver[123], but the King will not allow it to be sought

118. Cf. the statement above regarding Dona Cathrina.
119. See infra, D 2.
120. I do not know who these were. P. du Jarric, in his *Histoire* ii. 798 mentions a "king of Setecorlas" (Seven Korales), whose son was baptised by a Jesuit Father in 1607 or 1608, and who himself desired baptism; but no names are given.
121. The ed of 1617 has "Trinquamale."
122. Cf. supra, note 71. These galleys and *champanas* must have been purely State and pleasure boats for local use, as they would not have have gone farther down the Mahaweliganga, and certainly not upwards (see C. *Lit. Reg.* v 78 et seq.)
123. Very little gold, and no silver or copper, is found in Ceylon.

for. The precious stones, which are mostly in Candy, may not be sought for or traded in by any but in the presence of the King. If he desires any he causes search to be made for only as many as he just then wants: he gathers none for gain. The general persisted very stubbornly and strongly in regard to this, in order to be able to trade with him for a parcel of stones, but he would listen to nothing on the subject. He had also some special secret (reason) for this. In order to prevent our asking to trade with him for stones, he gave us some two hundred stones of all kinds, such as rubies, *bacan*[124], garnets and others, and said; "This I give you but I do not wish to sell any." So our general ceased from soliciting any more. Notwithstanding we got some good parcels here and there, but in a secret way. On the *play* of Matecalo many stones were offered for sale that had been brought secretly from Candy[125]. The aforesaid island is very rich in all kinds of precious stones and in many other materials, as before said, only it is not permitted that one seek and dig for them. I passed through some rivers where we took out the sand and washed it with clean water, in which we found garnets: yea, in the city of Candy whenever it has rained they searched in the drains in which the water runs, from which I have seen divers stones obtained, but they had to bring them all to the King. The country has much crystal. If one dig therein one will find many kinds of riches, such as crystal, many metals and other things, if they might be taken out. It has also much fine stone serving for building much good and suitable wood for making ships and houses, also many places where they have their salt. So that this island is certainly the most fruitful of which one can speak or write. It is suitable for planting and sowing all that is raised in other countries, such as oil, wheat and wine, all can grow well if it be planted or sown there, as we found by experience, and drank of the wines that grow there.[126] It has also plenty of cotton, divers wood and other roots for making dyes, ginger, tur-

124. See supra, note 26.
125. Cf. Supra.
126. See supra, note 50.

meric *cardomoma* and *mirrabelanes* can grow well there, we also found some nuts with *folie* or *mases*[127]. It is also a very healthy country and pretty temperate in atmosphere and heat. So that in this island there is nothing lacking for the needs of the body. Above all is to be deplored that they lack the highest thing the knowledge of God through Jesus Christ. It is to be hoped the Lord will grant them better knowledge, because they are a people that are very patient, not stiffnecked: one may freely tell them all their need and they are quite willing to be instructed. Even if they are convinced that their idolatry avails nothing, which one may freely say to them, they will answer you friendly that that it is the custom of the country, yea they often acknowledge that their idols are of no value. Dona Cathrina visits no *pagodes*[128]. Don Joan the King what he does is mostly to please the Singales. To the aforesaid island of Celon resort many pilgrims who visit the mountain of Adam, to view the footsteps of Adam, whither Don Joan himself once went, and caused the measurement of the footsteps to be placed in Candy[129]. When they have their festival much offering is made there. By such means the King knows how to get the money from the Singales, begins and builds many *pagodes*; some he allows to remain unfinished, for which he often causes contributions to be given, and all the same they remain unfinished. The money that mostly circulates there is silver *larins*, [130] also gold and silver *fannons*[131].

The great *pagodes* that one sees as one sails from Pointo de Gallo to Matecalo near the second shoals,[132] the aforenamed king once journeyed there in order to view the great

127. Mace (see *Hobson-Jobson* s.v.). *Foelie* is the Dutch name, which seems to be derived from an Indo-Port. *Fula* (flower, blossom) -Konkani *pula*, Hind, *phul*.

128. Cf. supra, note 61.

129. See the description of Ceylon at the end of Bree's Journal.

130. The ed. of 1617 has "laurins."

131. See *Hobson-Jobson* s.v. "Fanam."

132. On the map is drawn a large dagoba inland between Adam's Peak and some hills north of Dondra: this is described as "White showing *pagoda grande*." At "Trincoli" (Tirukkovil) a dagoba is also shown; and this seems to be the one referred to here (cf. infra), or there may be confusion with the Katāragama devale.

image that starts therein in the form of a man standing straight upright with a bare sword in his hand, his arm, raised to strike. This aforenamed King ere he journeyed to the *pagode* had many a time jested about the great image, but when he came into the great *pagode* that sword of the great personage's shook and rattled. The King seeing this was terrified. This the Singales relate as having so happened, the which the devil through his magicians and idol-servers can bring to pass[133]. This country is full of these horrors. The Singales believe firmly that the world will not perish as long as this *pagode* continues to stand. In Candy they have their images of deceased men, especially of their great lords. One sees a horrible thing there when they feel ill or unwell: at once they hasten to an image like a devil, to which they offer, for which purpose they always have in their houses a basket in which they collect that which they offer to the devil, and pray to be helped by him. In other places in Celon they pray much to an

---

133. Sir Thos. Herbert (*A relation of Some Yeares Travaile* 1634, p. 190) has the following quaint and incorrect version of the above :—" Pilgrims from remote parts apace flocke hither, where a top a high mount (sic!) is conspicuously set the *Idaea* of a horrible *Caco-demon*, touching which *Pagod*, the *Syngales* (their Priests) Cronography. (*sic*). That once *Iohna* (*sic.*) their king held this monstrous *Doemon* in derision, but entring the sacred Temple, he (in great agonie) beheld the Idoll Devill breath forth fury against him, shewing it by his fiery eyes and flaming semiter (threatfully held against him), whereat the relenting king amazed returnes, becomes penitentiary, and ecchoes sorrow for his former errours." In the second (revised and enlarged) edition (1638) the foregoing assumes the following form :—"They have many other Cacodemons horrible and ugly. The more deformed the more exact *Idaeas* of Devills, and the more venerable. A notable one is that (not farre from *Mattacala* conspicuous in its standing, an Idoll of great bulk and antiquity ; of which, the Singales and Joques Cronography. (sic). That, many years agoe, one *Iohna* (*sic.*) their King nourisht a ridiculous and impious conceit of this *Diabola*, as a foolish and senselesse Idoll. But loe, the Jogues by the Devills craft so wrought that upon a solemne day, as *Iohna* entred, he beheld the Pagod to breath out fire and furie, his eyes colur'd with rage, and the semiter in his had wrathfully bent against him ; the amazed King cryes out for help accuses his infidelity, confesses it a perfect Devill, and having well satisfied for his errour, is recouncil'd, and ever after a zealous Idolater." Knighton (1 327 n.), in quoting a third and later version, and laboring under the common delusion that " Matecalo " was Batticaloa (Puliyantivu,) thinks that Sir T. Herbert alludes to the Seruvila dagoba, which is situated to the north of the Verukal branch of the Mahaweliganga (see H. Parker's *Ancient Ceylon* 331.).

elephant's head made of wood or stone: they say that they do this to obtain wisdom[134]. Their errors and abominations are many there. It were to be wished that some Christian potentates would take the trouble to root out this idolatry from them, which would be quite practicable with God's help if one would take up the matter earnestly to the honour of God. For they are a people that willingly let themselves be instructed, and take well their errors being punished, without opposing it in anger. It might be said, that the Portuguese have laboured long to this end and effected nothing: in truth the Portuguese seek more the riches of Celon than true conversion or the knowledge of God through Jesus Christ.

As the King of Candy is a very shrewd worldly-wise man, who himself willingly hears all particulars of our countries in matters both of politics and religion, whereof our general many a time spoke with the aforenamed King, seeing him disposed towards our nation, our general, in hope of expecting some good, left with the aforenamed King a young man named Erasmus Martsbergher, who had studied somewhat and was fluent in many languages, and also of good life. The King took this as a great honour that the aforenamed Martsbergher was willing to remain there with him, and made him his secretary...Our general was well satisfied with the aforesaid Martsbergher, but (with) the great hope and probability of getting the King to abondon his heathenish errors, the aforenamed Martsbergher remained there, who promised to constantly make the King realize what abominations their *pagodes* are, and to beg the King to abandon them, and to bring him to the knowledge of God.[135]

The island of Celon was formerly large, being reckoned in circumference four hundred miles, but now quite forty miles have been taken away by the sea on the north-west side, so that the size or circumference is now reckoned three hundred miles [136]; and it has many convenient harbours,

134. The reference is to Ganesa, the god of wisdom. Sir T. Herbert (v. s.) refers to this statement also.

135. See supra, page 379 and infra.

136. The curtailment of Ceylon by the sea is referred to by many writers (cf C. A. S. Jl. xx. 32, 83).

of which the best is Poincte de Galle, a very convenient place for all large and small ships to trade from there to all the countries of the whole East Indies. This is a place as well situated as any to be found in the East Indies for interfering, [137] so that the Portuguese should in no wise be able to trade freely [138].

Hereunder follow the names of the most important places, how far they are situated from each other [139].

From Poincte de Galle, westwards [140].

Alican	9 miles
Verberir	1 mile
Calutre	3 miles
Coulombo	6 miles
Negombo	5 miles
tGilau	5 miles
Putalon	10 miles
Mannar	18 miles

From Poincte de Galle to Matecalo, eastwards [141]

Bellingan	4 miles
Mature	2 miles
Dondoure	1 mile
Tannadar	1 mile
Halpilana	2½ miles
Aialle	3 miles

137. In orig. *troubleeren*, from Fr. *troubler*.

138. Cf. infra.

139. Except in the case of the places between Matecalo and Candy, the distances given must have been obtained at second hand. Taking the mile here as equal to 4 miles English, the distances are fairly approximate, though in some cases rather inaccurate.

140. In this light the only names that need explanation are Alican—Alutgama, Verber—Beruwala, and tGilau—Chilaw.

141. In this list some of the names are very difficult to identify, and, beyond Dondra, the distances given are inaccurate, especially that between Metacalo and Trinquamale, the actual distance being about three times that given here. "Tannadar" seems to represent Gandara; "Halpilana" may mean Hambantota; "Aialle" looks like Yala, but, from the mileage, appears to be intended for (Maha) Lewaya; "Velebe," on the other hand, which ought to represent Walawe, by the mileage stands for Yala; "Tansalier" is a hopeless corruption, impossible of identification, though, by the mileage, it should be Kumbukkanara; "Trincoly" is Tirukkovil (see supra, note 10).

Velebe	9 miles
Tansalier	7 miles
Trincoly (a Pagoda)	12 miles
Matecalo	5 miles
Trinquamale	10 miles

These abovenamed places are situated on the sea-coast.

Here follow the places from Coulombo to Candy[142].

Tranquero Grando	3 miles
Malevano	2 miles
Grovabley	3 miles
Setavacca	3 miles
Grovenelle	2 miles
Manieratuate	4 miles
Dively	3 miles
Matappety	2 miles
Altonnor	1 mile
Ganiattany	1 mile
Ballene	1 mile
Candy	1 mile

From Matacalo to Candy[143].

Aldea de More	1½ mile
Oncattoty	2 miles
Viado	2 miles

---

142. Most of the names in this list are easily recognisable. "Tranquero grando" should be Tranqueira grande (Port), the great stockade" of Kaduwela (see C. A. S. Jl. xx. 286 n. 6); "Malevano" is Malwana, "Grovabley" is Gurubewila (Hanwella), "Grovenelle" is Ruwanwella, "Manicratuate" (a misreading for Manicravate) is Menikkadawara, "Dively" is Diwela, "Mattappety" is Attapitiya (perhaps confused with Mottappoliya), "Altonnor" is Alutnuwara, and "Ganiattany" is Ganetenna.

143. On the places in this list from "Neguritti" onwards see above, note 36 *et. seq.* "Aldea de more" (Moorish village) may be the Moorish portion of Sammanturai. "Oncattoty" is puzzling: the only name approaching it is Sungaturai, but this place is too far out of the way. "Viado" may be Verayadi. All these names, with their original erroneous spelling, are found in Dutch and other maps of Ceylon down to the latter part of the 18th century (the location, however, in some cases varying). The last survival is found in the map of 1803 in Percival's *Ceylon*, where we find "Vendre," placed *north* of Kandy, on the road to Trincomalee!

Neguritti	..	..	.. 5 miles
Nilvaele	..	..	.. 2 miles
Vegamme	.	..	.. 4 miles
Vintane	..	..	.. 6 miles
Vendro	..	..	.. 5 miles
Candy	..	..	.. 4 miles

So the 3rd September we departed from the island of Celon, from the *play* named Matecalo; and on the voyage to Achien nothing special befell us[144].

When our general told them [145] that he had lately been in the island of Celon in the roadstead of Matecalo, and had had the courage to journey so far into the country to the kingdom of Candy, where he had treated and spoken with the King of Candy, Fimala Darma Suriada, otherwise in the Christian fashion named Don Ian Daustria, bringing from there about 60 cannasters of cinnamon and some pepper, also many precious stones and presents in token of friendship, on hearing this they considered it to be no small matter because they highly esteem the aforesaid King of Candy, who has the courage to wage war on the Portuguese, as before related.

Anno 1603.

The 1st January our general went on shore again, speaking with the aforesaid King [146] in regard to the King of Candy, of his circumstances, how he waged war against the Portuguese, relating all that our general had transacted with the aforesaid King, which seemed to be agreeable to him: because the King of Achien afterwards sent ambassadors

144. They arrived at Achin on 16th September (see infra, D 2) and found lying in the road their pinnace the *Lam*, which they had lost off the Comoro Island in the night of 4th April, and the captain of which, Cornelis Specx, despairing of their arrival, and for other reasons, had agreed with the English general James Lancaster, that the latter should take her over, crew and all.

145. The Portuguese captain and officers of a big carrack that the English and Dutch had lain in wait for and captured in the Strait of Malacca on 13th October. Having been emptied of everything of value, she was, on account of bad weather, released on 20th October with all the Portuguese that had been in her; and before parting some conversation took place, in the course of which occurred the passage here quoted.

146. of Achin.

to the King of Candy; [147] so that it is not to be doubted that the king of Candy will obtain help and assistance from the King of Achien [148].

The 17th ditto (January 1603) there arrived in the roadstead of Achien two ships from Zeelant, the one named *Vlissinghen* and the other *der Goes*, (which) came from the roadstead of Matecalo from Celon, where they had left the ship *Ziericzee*, waiting for their clerk Sebalt de Weert, who had gone to the king of Candy, because he had learnt in Matecalo that our general had been there and had been well received, which made him resolve to go to the aforesaid King of Candy [149].

Meanwhile there arrived (5th February, 1603) the ship *Ziericzee* from Matecalo, wherein was Sebault de Weert, who had been in Candy, where much honour and friendship had befallen him. Ere he came to Candy he received letters from Erasmus Martsbergher, the clerk of our general left there, and now secretary to the King of Candy, from which letters the aforesaid Sebalt de Weert was able to settle how he had to act in Candy, because it was a great help to him that these persons had been left there by our general [150].

The 3rd April we departed from Achien........... The vice-admiral Zebalt de Weert in company of seven ships set out for Celon, saying adieu to the others by firing guns in their honour [151].

The same evening (27th April) our general sailed [152] to the aforesaid island (Dovo Poelo), coming about a bare mile from Bantam, taking with him various letters that Sr. [153] Zebalt de Weert, vice-admiral, had given him to deliver into the hands of the admiral aforesaid (van Warwijk). On coming to the island to the admiral Warwijck he was greatly welcomed, and they were all glad to hear the

147. See infra, D 2.
148. The writer had no prevision of the terrible disaster that was so soon to occur in Ceylon.
149. See infra, C 1.
150. See infra, C 1.
151. See infra D 2.
152. From Bantam, where he had arrived that day.
153. *Sinjeur* (from Port. *Senhor*).

good arrival of their companions in Achien, and how they had left again for Celon.

The 13th August there arrived before Bantam the ship named *Dergoes* of Zeelandt, the skipper of which was Pieter Jansz. Soet and the upper merchant Jaques van Ray, who came from Celon [154]. but brought (God better it) very bad tidings of the vice-admiral Zebalt de Weert, namely [155] that he was murdered by the King of Candy near Matecalo with some 53 persons of his company, which is much to be wondered at, since our general had so often been entirely in the hands of the aforesaid King, and had received every friendship from the aforesaid King, as has been related above in this journal. On asking the aforesaid persons of the ship *Dergoes* what reason the King of Candy alleged for committing such a barbarous deed, they said that they considered the reason to be that they had let four Portuguese ships go with their crews which they had taken, and the *modeliar* Emanuel Dios, who was at Matecalo, asked of the vice-admiral some Portuguese and *mesticos* for the King of Candy, but it seems that they were refused him. They were indeed also warned by Reynier Janssz, a man of ours that had remained on shore there, [156] that they should let no Portuguese or their servants go, if they wished to expect any merchandise from the King of Candy. The King of Candy hearing these tidings of the capture of the Portuguese though he had meant to come no further than to Vintane, came to Matecalo, thinking to obtain the Portuguese there; but as soon as the vice-admiral with his broad council heard that the King was coming to Matecalo, they let the Portuguese with their servants and ships go free which the King having seen when he came to Matecalo caused him to form a very bad opinion, because he cannot understand that we mean well towards him, and are also enemies of the Portuguese as we declared to him, whilst we treat the Portuguese with courtesy and no enmity. The aforesaid King is a

---

154. Whence she had sailed on 20th June (see infra, D 2. s.d.).

155. Compare this account with the narratives of Bree and Rijcks infra

156. Apparently one of the two deserters mentioned above.

very jealous King, never trusting the Portuguese, and considers that hard measures should always be dealt out to them, as indeed mostly happens, because in the whole East Indies there is no King or nation that resists the Portuguese so inimically. That he is thus so jealous and knows all the tricks of the Portuguese, comes from the fact that he was brought up by the Jesuits in Goa and Colombo, as we have above related. Being at Matecalo, the vice-admiral received the King very magnificently with some 300 men all under arms. The King requested that the vice-admiral would give his men leave to return to the ships. It seems that the king did not take it well that anyone should come into his country with so many armed men, because (so we understood) the King appears to have said to the vice-admiral "We shall afterwards speak to one another alone;" so the armed men withdrew, the vice-admiral keeping with him some clerks, trumpeters, and other servants. Coming into discourse with the King through the interpreter Erasmus Martsbergher.[157] a man that was left by our general with the king, and now Secretary to the King, and well skilled in the Singales language, the King requested the vice-admiral to go to Pointo de Gallo with his ships, and the King would proceed thitherward over land with an army in order to capture Pointe de Gallo; which the vice-admiral was very willing to promise the king, but asked the king that he would come on board, which did not please the King, and he also begged to be excused; whereupon the vice-admiral said through the aforesaid interpreter, that if the King would not come on board he also would not go to Pointe de Gallo with the ships. Upon this reply the King said: "*Matta esto can*"[158]; whereupon followed the dreadful massacre. This is what we understood and heard from the persons on the aforesaid

157 This important statement is not made by the other narrators

158 Correctly, "*Mata este cao.*" ("Kill this dog"). Why the King should have given the order in Portuguese, instead of in Sinhalese, is not clear. The Maha Mudaliyar, Emanuel Dias, though a Portuguese by birth, was then to all intents a Sinhalese. Perhaps in his fury Vimaladharma relapsed into the language he had been accustomed to speak as Dom Joao de Austria. On Baldaeus' fiction see infra, F 5.

ship *Dergoes.* Our general was very grieved at these tidings, the misfortune of so many good friends, and also that now the good progress and friendship that our general had made with the aforesaid King should be brought to naught and destroyed; because our general has letters from the aforesaid King both to their honorable high mightiness the States and to His Excellency, begging therein for assistance to war against the Portuguese. We have not learnt otherwise whether Don Ian King in Candy is a genuine enemy of the Portuguese. During the time that we were in Celon we captured some Portuguese ships, as related above, one of which with her lading our general presented to the king of Matecalo. The *Modeliar* of Candy, Emanuel Dios, got as many Portuguese and *mesticos* as he desired, and sent them to the King of Candy, with also the best weapons that we found in the ships of the Portuguese; moreover our general caused a new galley and *champaignie* with their cargo of *arecca* to be set on fire, and that in order to prove to the Singales that we are enemies of the Portuguese.

For mercy to faithless Portuguese to show
Brings ourselves but pain and woe[159].

---

159. In origi.:—" Want deucht te doen aen Portugisen on trouw Brenght ons selven in druck en rouw."

To be continued.

THE EARLIEST DUTCH VISITS TO CEYLON

BY DONALD FERGUSON,

Continued from Vol: XXX, No. 80, p. 409

B. 2. LETTER FROM DUTCH MERCHANTS AT ACHIN TO DIRECTORS OF N. E. I. CO. IN HOLLAND, DATED 18, NOVEMBER, 1602 [1].

Laus Des, 18, November, 1602 in........[2] Joris Spilbergh arrived here on the 17th September [3], after he had put in to many places on the coast of Guinea, Amobon [4], the bay of Saldaingna [5], the river of Cuama [6], Mallelle in the Commorros [7], and Seylon[8] ......In coming hitherward he put in to the roadstead of Matecallo, and journeyed 32 miles inland to Don Juan, King of Candi, with whom he treated much, left two men with him, and received and bought from him many precious stones and some cinnamon, but the worth of the stones we do not know, although they estimate them highly [9].

......Your honor's obedient servants,
CORNELIS JOLYT, NICOLAES PIETERS, JAN MAERSSE, LUCAS ANTHONISZ[10].

1. The extract here given is copied from a document in the India office *Hague Transcripts* (First series 1. viii). The writers of the letter had been left at Achin by the ships of the Middleburg Company (see *supra* No. 80 p. 369) in order to establish a Dutch factory there.
2. This blank is in the copy; but the original probably had " Atsien " (Achin).
3. See supra.
4. Read " Annobon."
5. Saldanha Bay, which Spilbergen renamed "Table Bay."
6. The name by which the Portuguese called the Zambesi.
7. Mohilla, one of the Comoro Islands (see supra).
8. On the above see *C. Lit. Reg.*, vi. 309.
9. For details of Spilbergen's visit to Ceylon see supra, B1.
10 The Spilbergen diarist mentions these men under 17, September, 1602, by the names of "Cornelis Jolijt, Jan Mertsz, Lucas *Jansz*, and Claes Pieterssen," and under 29th, January, 1603, mentions " Klaes Pieterssz of Flushing and Lucas *Jansz* of Antwerp." De Jonge, however (*Opkomst,* iii 398) gives the names as in this letter.

C. SEBALT DE WEERT'S ACCOUNT OF HIS FIRST VISIT TO CEYLON, IN A LETTER TO WYBRAND VAN WARWYCK, DATED AT ACHIN, 1st APRIL, 1603.

Of this lengthy letter, which was utilized by de Jonge in his *Opkomst, iii*, there is a copy in the India Office *Hague Transcripts* (First Series I)., and it is from this that I have made my translation. Neither de Jonge, nor anyone else, as far as I know, has drawn attention to the fact that the account of de Weert's first visit to Ceylon, as published by the brothers de Bry in 1605, 1606, &c. (see *infra*, D2, introduction) is simply an almost literal translation of the summary contained in the document described hereafter (see D1, note 1), which summary, internal evidence proves, was made from this very letter. The Spilbergen diarist tells us (supra) that de Weert's letters to admiral van Warwÿck were delivered to the latter at Bantan on 27th April, 1603, by Spilbergen (*cf. infra*); and it is evident that this letter, or a copy of it, was sent home by van Warwyck by the combined fleet under Heemskerck and Spilbergen, which reached Holland on 24th March, 1604 (see *infra*). The anonymous summarizer has done his work well on the whole, though he has passed over some of the most interesting portions of de Weert's letters : a fair idea of this may be gained from the notes I have appended to the translation. From these also can be judged how closely the German version of de Bry follows the Dutch summary ; but this will be seen even more clearly if we place in parallel columns the opening paragraphs of the Dutch summary and of de Bry's translations.

DS.	DB.
Coming further to the 14 ships and one yacht that sailed under the command of the admiral Wÿbrandt van Warwÿck and vice admiral Sebolt de Weert, of these the three named *Zirckzee*, *Vlissingen* and *Der Goes*, under the command of the vice admiral Sebolt de Weert arrived the 28	This voyage of the abovesaid Sebold de Weert will moreover be more fully described, and in substance is shortly as follows : that he arrived the 28 November anno 1603 [*sic*] off the island of Zeylon and that

November a° 1603 [*sic*] off the island of Seylon. The vice admiral betook himself with 15 men on land and was there well received and brought with 6 elephants to Matacalou, from there pursuing his journey with 6 men to the chief city Candij, situated 36 miles inland, where the great king holds his court. Owing to rain and bad weather he was 15 days on the way, finding in every place very friendly and obliging people, who treated him and his [men] very well and defrayed [them] of all expenses.

he betook himself with 15 persons on land, where he was then well received, and brought with 6 elephants to Matecalo. From there he took his journey further with 6 persons to the chief city Candy, situated some 30 or 40 miles inland, where the great king holds his court: owing to much rain and bad weather he had to be 15 days long on the way where he met everywhere a very friendly people, who received [and] treated him and his [men] full friendly and well, and defraying [them] of all expenses.

But, if it is evident that the de Brys had in their possession a copy of this summary it is equally clear that they also had access to the full text of de Weert's letter (at a later date, probably), since, as I show elsewhere (D2, introduction, note[1]), they utilized, in an interpolation to Bree's diary, portions of the letter that the Dutch summarizer had passed over.

LETTER FROM SEBALD DE WEERT AT ACHIN TO WYBRAND VAN WARWIJCK AT BANTAM.

Most honored, wise, very prudent sirs [*sic*], . : The reasons that move us to go to Seylon I shall relate at length to your honor, together with what befell me there, [and] I beg your honor to take in good part my prolixity in writing, [since it] is in order that your honor may the better have knowledge of the kingdomof Zeylon, and receive favorably and approve of our effort.

After we had arrived with fair prosperity off the island of Zeylon at the altitude of about 7 degrees we went on shore at a place named Panem [2], where we learnt that Mattacalou where we wished to be lay about 10 or 12 miles[3] higher,

1. On 28th November, 1602, (see infra, D2). It will be noticed that throughout this letter de Weert gives no dates.

2. Sic, a copyist's error for "Panane" (cf. infra, D2, note 38).

3. If the mile here mentioned be taken as equal to 4 miles English, the distance given is fairly correct, from Pānawa to Karativu being about 48 miles by the present coast road.

and that there had been there two large ships, the which by tokens they gave me of the captain as also of others I found to have been the general Spilbergen, the bearer of this [4], who had been up inland to Candy, where the great king resides [5], that he had also left there four men [6], and further that he had further laden for home, at which we were not a little rejoiced. In Mattacalou[7] I heard the same; but as we were made to believe much regarding lading, and two clerks remaining on land saw no appearance thereof, we resolved to set sail again direct for Achin, and making ready therefor, there came the message from the king[8] that we should not depart before we had sent a man or two to Candy to the great king, who could well lade us, that in the country there was plenty of pepper, wax[9] and cinnamon, and all reasonably cheap; also a great quantity of precious stones; on hearing which, we changed our resolution, and arranged that two ships[10] alone should depart, in order to advise those of Achin of our intention, and that, I remaining there should myself go to Candy lying about 36 miles inland[11], and not be deceived by evil reports.

So I went ashore, taking with me some presents for the king, and as it was winter[12] there, and was bad weather daily, our boat was thrown over by the breakers right from stern to stern, and I that could not swim right under it, but God be praised we suffered no harm except to our goods. (During all the time we lay there also we did not lose one man, though very seldom any boat or canoe went to land

4. See supra, B1, and infra, D2.

5. Cf. supra. B1,

6. Two he had left at Kandy (see supra, No. 80 p. 388 and two had deserted at Matecalo (see supra,). No. 80 p. 385

7. Not the town, which lay some miles inland, and which de Weert did not visit until later (see infra), but the road or shore of Matecalo, where de Weert arrived probably next day (29th November).

8. See supra.

9. After "wax" the copy has "quan" (?), which I cannot explain.

10. The *Vlissingen* and *der Goes*, which sailed for Achin on 11th December, 1602 (see supra, B1, and infra, D2.)

11. Cf. supra, p. 57, where de Bry interpolates after 36 "or 40."

12. That is the north-east monsoon period.

that was not upset or filled). Coming on land[13] we were well received, and immediately rode with six elephants to Mattacalou[14] about a mile inland[15], where we were shown great honour by the king, and he begged much that I would be willing to send someone to Candÿ, [and] he would meanwhile cause to be collected all the pepper, wax and cinnamon that was possible to him, doubting not that within three months he would load us: but he is a cheat who has very little power, is tributary to the Portuguese, and obedient to the king of Candij more from constraint than good-will[16]. His hope was, that through the daily bad weather our ship should come to be wrecked, whereby he would have got a booty, though he feigned himself otherwise[17].

Having waited quietly there one day, I sent on board again a part of the crew (because I had 15 men with me), and with six men set out on the journey upon elephants. On the way we had daily so much rain that we were fifteen days on the journey, often prevented by the rivers from pursuing the journey. On the road I found such friendly and obliging people that it is incredible: we were everywhere defrayed[18] and well treated. On coming halfway, there met us seven men, who were sent by the king, as he had tidings that there were three ships on the coast, in order to learn what ships they were, who were very·[glad][19] at seeing us, they brought letters from the Dutch that were in Candÿ[20], [and] begged that we would be pleased to write

13. Probably on the day that the other ships sailed (11th December).

14. Cf. Spilbergen's reception. The *town* of Matecalo is now spoken of.

15. So also the Spilbergen diarist. Bree says "full two miles," and Rÿcks "a short mile." The present town of Chammanturai lies between three and four miles from the sea, so that Rÿcks seems nearest the mark.

16. Cf. supra.

17. Of course de Weert knew nothing at that time of the unfriendly conduct that this chief had shown towards Spilbergen. All the diarists agree in their condemnation of the vanniya of Matecalo.

18. The copy has "gedesnoijeert," evidently an error for "gedefroÿeert" (cf. infra, note 95). Ds. as printed has the form "defrezeerden," which seems to be a misleading for "defroÿeerden."

19. This word is wanting in the copy.

20. Cf. the statement of the Spilbergen diarist, supra.

what people we were, because the king desired it much; whereupon they immediately sent back two men with the answer, other two forward to view my ship, and the rest remained with me. The king having received my letters was so delighted that he could not keep patience, longing so for my coming that he could not rest, he sent me every hour people with victuals, refreshments [21] and every token of benevolence; he also sent his brother-in-law[22] with 100 men with pipes and drums to receive and convoy me. On coming near the city I was received with such magnificence and triumph that I know not if in our land one could do more after the manner of the country to his princely excellency. When we were two days' journey from the city he sent his own *palankin*[23], in which I was carried[24].

On coming into the city, the people were all astir[25] the soldiers[26] in order quite half a mile along the road through which I must pass; all the ordnance was fired, [and] they made such a noise of[27] trumpets, shawms and such like instruments[28], that one could neither see nor hear[29]. Thus I was conducted to my lodging, which was behung according to custom[30], whilst the king sent me word that I should rest a little and thereafter come and speak with him; but I had hardly the leisure in which I could eat something, [when he] summoned me immediately to him, [and] gave me no [time] to dress myself and make ready my presents.

---

21. De Bry alters this to "fruits."

22. This must have been a brother of one of Vimaladharma's sub-queens (cf. supra, B1, note 35).

23. DB. interpolates here "or litter, that had to be carried by several persons."

24. Compare the preceding and what follows with the description of Spilbergen's reception, supra.

25. This, I think, is the meaning here, though "op de weere" might be translated "on their defence." Ds. has "the burghery was all afoot" (op de been); while DB. has "the burghers of the city were all mustered" (aufgeinahuct).

26. DB. interpolates "with their weapons."

27. DS. (and DB.) interpolates "drums."

28. DS. (but not DB.) interpolates "also of the ordnance."

29. Compare Linschoten i. 228, 258 (where the English translation is faulty).

30. DS. "suitably behung and adorned" DB. "right stately behung and adorned."

I was again conducted to the court with such playing[31], and number of people that we could hardly get unhindered along the street. My presents were carried uncovered before me, which were, a red cloth, two large mirrors, a handsome gilt musket, a beautiful gilt sword that I had taken with me for my own use, and further a lot of handsome glasses, but mostly broken on the way In the hall, which, though with us it would not have been of much consequence, nevertheless I consider to be handsomer than [those] of any kings of all these islands, [and] was made in no wise after our or the Portuguese manner[32],—stood all those of his council and captains[33] on each side against the wall. In the middle hung the likeness of his princely excellency[34] painted on a cloth full-size from life, presented to the king a little before by the general Spelbergen[35], and a handsome carpet spread in front of it, on which my presents were laid. At the side in a little recess stood the king leaning against the wall, having in front of him two children, son and daughter[36], rightful heirs to the country. Having come before him and greeted him in the manner of our country, with one knee on the ground[37], he having told me at once to rise and bidden me welcome through an interpreter deplored greatly the inconvenience that I had suffered on his behalf on such a far journey and in such weather. He asked me whence and why I came, to which I replied, I came from a country called by the Portuguese Frandes[38], which was several provinces

31. DS. (and DB.) "noise of shawms."

32. The Spilbergen diarist appears not to have been struck with the appearance of the hall of audience, at least, he says nothing of it (see supra).

33. DS. (and DB.): "captains of war."

34. DS. "his excellency Mauritius of Nassau." DB. "his excellency count Moritz of Nassaw."

35. See supra.

36. DS. has: "his son the young prince, 3 years old, and his daughter 6 years old." DB. follows this, but puts the ages in words, and erroneously makes the daughter "eight years old." (Cf, infra, notes 78 and 81.) The Spilbergen diarist (supra,) mentions these children, but does not tell us how old they were. If de Weert is correct in his estimates, the girl must have been born in 1596, and the boy in 1599. Baldaeus says (see infra F5) that when Dom Joao died in 1604 he left a son and two daughters.

37. DS. (and DB.): "with bended knees."

38. DS. "Flanders." DB. "Flandern."

confederated together and governed by the nobles of the country, whom we call *los estados*[39], under the command of our prince[40] whose likeness was hanging there. On saying which, there was great gladness among his lords[41], because I recognized the likeness of his princely excellency, since thereby he found the statement of the general Spelbergen, who had been there just four months before[42], to be true, and that we were from one country; because to that end was the likeness hung there. I said further to him that we were merchants (who had) come there to buy cinnamon, pepper, precious stones and other wares, and to sell ours, seeking the friendship of all kings and princes of the countries and islands of India, in order to be able to trade freely with their subjects, that we had for several years now had intercourse with Atchin, Bantam and the Moulucas, and were great friends of the kings, since we were enemies of the Portuguese, and that for over thirty[43] years now we[44] had warred with the king of Portugal[45], that we also had commission and command from our prince to assist and help all kings and princes that were expelled by the Portuguese. Whereupon immediately interrupting and breaking my recital, as he not only understands but also speaks Portuguese well, and has no need of interpreter except for honour's sake—he had me told that I had come at an opportune time, and that God had sent me there as to a king that more than

39. The States (general). De Weert seems to have thought that the king, knowing Portuguese, would understand the Spanish term.

40. DS. (and DB.) has: "which were ruled by the gentlemen the states of the same lands, and his princely excellency."

41. DS. (and DB.) includes the king in the display of joy.

42. DS. has "Spilberghen," omits "just four months," and interpolates: "had declared many things, and presented the likeness to the king." DB. follows this, but omits "had declared many things."

43. D.B. "twenty."

44. Instead of "we" DS. has "the gentlemen the States and his excellency's forefather of most praiseworthy memory and his excellency," which DB. expands still further into "....his father of blessed and of most praiseworthy memory Wilhelmus the first prince of Vranien [*sic*, for Oranien=orange], and count of Nassaw, &c."

45. DS. interpolates "and still did," which DB expands to 'and still waged through his son count Mauritius"

any others was annoyed by the Portuguese, who contrary to right and reason wished to take away his country from him and drive him out[46], he begged accordingly that I would execute my commission and carry it into effect as early as possible. To which I replied that there was no doubt that God had brought me there, but it was not by chance,as one says, because I had come there by express command of our prince, who, having heard of the continuous wars that the kings of Ceylon (without knowing of Candy or of [47]) had against the Portuguese, had sent me there to form alliance and friendship with the king, [and] to promise him help and assistance ; but that his majesty well knew that no princes or rulers gave anyone assistance to their own loss,—that we came from so far at great trouble and expense, that if in his country there was any probability of lading, help should not be wanting to him ; that he should accordingly arrange to have pepper planted, and every year Dutch ships would come there ; that he would now lade me, so that I might immediately sail home and return again with assistance. This he promised to do, on condition that I would wait there four months, because he must have the pepper brought from the mainland, seeing that there was very little pepper there, even though he should sell all his elephants therefor.

Upon this I took my leave in order to go to my lodging promising to come again to his majesty the next day when it pleased him to summon me. But when I thought to depart, the king called me back, and bade ask me how I was so bold that I durst hazard to come so far into his country, without knowing him or having advice[48] from him and

46. Instead of what follows, to the end of the paragraph, DS. (followed by D.B.) has : " he therefore begged that the vice-admiral would assist him by water, to the end that those from Goa might effect no supply or relief. By land he would go with 20,000 men to seek the Portuguese in their strongholds. To which was answered that the costs of the ships and the men (coming from such far countries) was [*sic*] very great, and that his majesty must make a suitable recompense for the requested help, whereupon the king made many excellent offers, saying also that he was of such a will." This is hardly on accurate summary of de Weert's account, and brings in out of its place a passage that occurs in a later portion of the letter.

47. Sc in the copy. What *word* should fill the blank, I do not know : perhaps " him."

48. DS. (and DB.) :" Consent."

some hostages. To which I answered that many reasons had moved me thereto, but that the principal of them were the Portuguese. Being astonished at this, he asked, how that was possible, seeing that I had declared that they were our enemies, and that I also well knew that he was an enemy of the Portuguese, he did not know how he should understand that. Whereupon I immediately replied that this was the very reason, which the Portuguese gave me, to embolden me to come so far into his country, without first advising him of my arrival. I omitted to ask permission, because I was confident that a king that was a real enemy of the Portuguese must necessarily be a friend of our, likewise enemies of the same Portuguese, and that coming unexpectedly to such a king I should be all the more welcome; that I should also well avoid venturing such in other countries. At this there was great laughter[49], and the king asked me what were the other reasons that had moved me thus to come to him. Upon which I answered, in the first place, the honour, courtesy and good treatment that he had accorded to the general who had been there before me[50], who had come thence so freely; in the second place, that I should be ashamed not to dare venture what another had done before me[51], and lastly, the honour that the king of Mattacalou had shown me on arrival and the good-will that I saw that the common people had towards us. Hereupon the king asked again if I trusted in the people so readily, seeing I had not spoken to the general himself. I answered, yes, as the words of many persons in different places agreed well, because it is not very possible that many persons in speaking do not contradict each other, if the matter is not as they wish to have it understood, the more so in that these people had had no time (not knowing of our arrival) to be suborned.

With this the king well satisfied let me depart to my lodging, where were brought immediately so many pots

---

49. By abbreviating the foregoing, DS. (and DB.) makes the laughter seem somewhat out of place.

50. DS. " general Spilbergen." "DB". " general von Spilbergen."

51. DS. (and DB.) omits the second reason.

with all kinds of whey, panades[52], conserves, fruits and other confections[53], that I found the house far too small; also a majordomo with four male and three[54] female slaves to serve us. When I was in the house, all the principal lords came to visit me and bid me welcome. [The king] also sent me immediately 50 *larins* (which are like pieces of eight[55]) to spend.

Towards the evening the king again summoned me to him in order to speak with me alone. On coming up I found him walking about, having only three or four of his privy council with him; and when I offered to kiss his hands, he took me in his arms and squeezed me heartily[56], so that he made my ribs crack (I had much rather have been embraced by a pretty maiden[57]), meaning thereby to show how welcome I was to him. He at once asked me if I had no letter of credence from my prince, which having produced,—he had it brought [to him] and a seal of his excellency's[58] that the general Spelbergen had left with him, with the warning that whoever did not bring such a token was not of our people[59], with which having compared[60] mine, and finding that they were both alike, he was greatly rejoiced[61], and at once promised me to make every exertion to lade my

52. Panade or panada is an old name for a kind of broth (see *New English Dictionary*, s.v.).

53. DS. in place of " confections " has " eatables." Ds. omits " whey panades," and has " delicious conserves and preserved fruits.

54. DB. omits " three."

55. After " *larins* " DS. (and DB.) inserts "silver," and in place of the words in brackets DB. has " which are long silver coins " (or " pence ").

56. As he had done to Spilbergen (see supra,).

57. DS. (and of course DB.) omits this parenthetical remark, which was scarcely intended " for public consumption."

58. DS. interpolates " count Mauritz."

59. The Spilbergen diarist does not mention this fact. DB. alters the foregoing to " a letter and seal that he had previously received from his excellency count Moritz."

60. DS. interpolates " and scrutinizing very sharply."

61. Here DS. summarizes a great deal of what follows in the words " saying : if they of Flandres would continue their navigation to his realms, in order to negotiate, all fruits of cinnamon, pepper and other wares should be for them alone, that he would also let them sail to other places and to the mainland and trade with recommendation to many kings, some being of his kindred and others his good friends." DB. follows this, with a few verbal differences. The Dutch version in *Begin ende Voortganghhas* " silk [!] pepper, cinnamon," &c.

ships within four months ; he was also sorry that I had sent away my two other ships[62], because he would have liked to lade them all together. Whereupon I made my excuse that we were destined to Achin, where our general[63], with thirteen other ships[64] was to come ; that through fear that the latter should wait for us I had sent two ships thitherward in order to advise him of my arrival, as I did not think that there would have been lading there for all our ships ; that Atchijn was our rendezvous, whence the ships were to be sent to various places [65]; that if he could not help me earlier than within four months, it were better that I also went to Atchijn, and come back in four months, or sent another ship, the more so, in that it was winter and very risky to lie on the coast. To which he answered that I need not fear, that I could safely moor the ship, [as] he had anchors and cables enough for me. At this I began laughing, and when he asked me why I laughed, I answered that I saw well that his majesty did not know what ships we had, but imagined that we had *champones*[66] or junks, that he was mistaken, because I should need to have for the lading of my ship at least 2,500 *baeren*[67] of pepper ; that I had on board 36 large cannon: which he would hardly believe, wherefore I begged that he would send one of his principal lords with me to view the same. At this the king being astonished immediately said that he had not imagined that my ship had been so big ; that he did not wish to deceive me or to delay me to no purpose, —that he did not know how to obtain any ladings for me, since the Portuguese had possession of his best land where the best cinnamon and pepper grew ; that he could probably procure 1,000 quintals within three months, but for so much pepper he knew of no expedient, that he was no merchant but a soldier, who thought

62. See supra. p. 58

63. The admiral, Wybrand van Warwyck.

64. That is, thirteen in addition to de Weert's ship, the *Zierickzee*.

65. See infra, D1, , and compare the end of this letter, where de Weert points out the superiority of Galle as a central port for the Dutch ships

66. See supra. No. 80, p. 387, note 71

67. Bahars (see *Hobson-Jobson*, s.s. " Bahar)."

neither of the building of a house, nor of planting, nor anything else by which he should be able to make profit, but only how he should protect his country; that no ships had even been there, and consequently he had had no experience in trade, but that his country was as suitable for yielding plenty of pepper as any in India: if he were master of his country, he would cause great plenty of pepper to be planted. As regarded cinnamon it grew of itself in the woods, [and] cost him only the trouble of levying on each village to furnish a certain quantity, desiring no money also therefor. If we would afford him any assistance, he would promise to furnish us every year with 1,000 quintals, and that for ever ana aye; and if we [captured] the fort of Punta de Gaela [he would give us] 2,000 quintals, and [if] Columbo, all the cinnamon of the whole country. He would also bind himself and all his successors that they should not be able to sell a pound of cinnamon to anyone in the world, but deliver all to us, and whatever else we might further stipulate. That I should consider the matter, because here was to be go. honour for myself and profit for our country. That with great trouble we sought to build forts in other places that were near his country, against the will of the inhabitants, that he himself now called and begged us thereto. He promised all help: if we were on the coast, he would at once take the field with 20,000 men, desiring of us no more than to prevent by water that any victual came into Columbo from Goa: he could easily press the enemy on land. He would give the captured forts into our care[68] (since his people were not fitted to take charge of forts), that from there we should be able to send our ships to all quarters, and always take our refuge[69] in a king who should be our friend and ally. That we would be willing to seize this occasion, because if he were expelled through lack of assistance, such an opportunity would not offer in

68. DS. (followed by DB.) has "into the hands of the states of Flanders."

69. DS. interpolates "in the aforesaid fortresses and" DB. has "fortress."

India in our lifetime[70], that we would therefore be pleased to hasten and take his affairs to heart, or otherwise he would have cause to complain at our arrival in his country, because the Portuguese would now attack him much harder than before, from fear that in time we might succour him; that the matter required haste; that the great trouble and expense that the Portuguese incurred in order to gain his country should serve us as a proof of the value of his country; that in the whole of India there was not so rich or so fruitful a country, nor [one] so well situated. That henceforth he wished to be called *Hermano en armas de sua ex timo principe dorange*[71], and other similar speeches in order to persuade me—who was only too greatly inclined thereto because of the great profits that our united masters would thereby be able to enjoy for so many years and the honour of our fatherland—to his help. To all of which foregoing reasons I answered him that such as he desired could with great difficulty be accomplished this voyage, that although we had many ships they were fitted out only for trade, and consequently not so provided with men that we should be able to put many men on land; that it was also uncertain if I should find the fleet still in Achin,—that it might have left before my arrival: that it were better that I should obtain my lading in haste, in order thus to sail home, and from there bring succour. To this he replied that his affairs did not admit of so long a delay; and that [as] I had come to-day, to-morrow I should rest, and the day after depart[72] And therewith he took a gold toothpick[73] from his neck, set with small garnets[74], worth about 6*f*[75], and hung it round my

70. DS. (and DB.) has "nevermore would such an opportunity occur to those of Flandres."

71. "Brother in arms of his excellency the prince of Orange." The Spanish is faulty, and is de Weerts' version of the interpreter's Portuguese.

72. All the foregoing is much abbreviated by DS. (and DB.)

73. This seems a strange and not very delicate present. The Sinhalese are not in the habit of using toothpicks; and if this really was one, Vimaladharma must have acquired the habit while with the Portuguese.

74. DS. (and DB.) omits this clause. The words I have translated "set" is in the copy "gegraviseert," which seems to be an error for "gegarniseert" (lit "garnished," i.e., adorned).

75. So written in the copy. DS. (and DB.) omits the value

neck and as it was dark, he let me go home, with the command to come to him as his guest the next day.

The third day he had me called to come and eat with him. Having come [there], as it was yet early, he chatted of various matters while walking about (because there it is not the custom to sit on the ground as in other countries: the kings when they speak to anyone, even of their own people, always stand, as also those that are near them). So I begged to see his children; and himself going in, he brought his daughter, about six years old[76], by the hand, with a gold cup full of wine made from the grapes that grow in his house[77], and presented [it] to me to drink. Having accepted the cup, I wished to kiss the young princess's hands, at which she being perplexed, since they are not wont to come near men, ran away crying out, and although her father called her several times, she would not come. Having drunk, I presented the cup back again, but he would not accept (it), saying that, seeing that his daughter had run away, I should take the cup with me; and as I refused this, he shut the door in my face.[78] Shortly afterwards he came again with the young prince, about three years old[79], on his arm, who offered me his hand and bade me welcome; and when I had kissed his hands, the father requested that I would take him under my protection and be his guardian, and not suffer that he who was the rightful heir to the country (because he had won the mother with the sword) should be driven out of it: the which I promised him to do according to my

---

76. DS. gives the age, but DB. omits it. (Cf. supra, note 36).

77. DS. (and DB.) omits the words after "wine," which are of importance in connection with the subject of the cultivation of the grape wine in Ceylon. (Cf. the not quite clear statements of the Spilbergen diarist, supra B1.) Vimaladharma was apparently pioneer of grape culture in the hill-country of Ceylon, though it is probable that the wine may have been introduced into the Island by the Portuguese sometime before. As a professed Buddhist, the king ought to have had nothing to do with the manufacture of strong drink. It is probable that he acquired the habit of drinking wine while with the Portuguese: whether he still continued it, is not apparent.

78. DS. (and DB.) omits the foregoing interesting details.

79. DS. gives the age, but DB. omits it (Cf. supra, note 36).

small power, and to recommend him to my prince[80]. Having heard this, the child drew from his side a little creese, with a silver sheath[81] (if it was by order of his father I do not know,) and presented it to me : at which I was so pleased that, having nothing else to give, I took from my side, with strap and all that belonged thereto, my sword[82], which with its accessories was worth over 20 pounds, and [which] I would not willingly have given to the father, even had he desired it of me, and presented it to the young prince ; and although the father somewhat deprecated it, since I had no other for the road, he held it in such worth that it is incredible : he also promised that it should be the first weapon that the prince should use when grown up[83]. After this[84] he confided to me how he had won with the sword the mother (who was the daughter of the preceding king and rightful heiress to the country), defeating 800 Portuguese, among them the general with all the captains, and bore as a token of the victory the representations of the heads in the clasps of his anklets. Because when the Portuguese had captured the city of Candij, and had defeated and expelled the King, who was the father of this daughter and a friend of the Portuguese[85], they brought the daughter, who had been brought up by them [and] baptized, as also the king, and was instructed in their faith, into Candij, with the intention to marry her (who was as yet only 12 years old) to a Portuguese nobleman. But Don Juan Doustria (so the king was called among the Portuguese, and so also he signs his letters —he was also so baptized, although afterwards he became a

80. DS. (and DB.) omits the foregoing.

81. DS. (and DB.) omits these four words.

82. In the copy "geweer," which usually means a musket, but here evidently a sword is intended. DS. (followed by DB.) has "Tydgeweer," side-arms.

83. DS. abbreviates all the foregoing into the statement : "the king saying, were my son old enough, I should have like to let him exercise with your prince." DB. follows this, but with a little more verbiage.

84. The whole of the rest of this paragraph, together with the next two, is omitted by DS. (and DB.).

85. I can explain the Dutch in no other way, but it certainly does not state the fact, since poor Dom Filippe was not driven out of Kandy by the Portuguese, nor, apparently was the father, but uncle, of Dona Catharina (see C.A.S. Jl. XX 389, 392).

heathen again) having been summoned by the inhabitants of the country as a defender as being a brave captain, they so harassed the Portuguese that they had to leave Candij, and in their departure they slew them all and took the queen prisoner, whom he married against her inclination, as she did not wish to have him, because he was black and she was white, also because he being a christian had more wives. But nevertheless the king proceeded therewith, and has now these two children by her[86].

Having chatted on these and other matters, it was time for eating, wherefore the king retired within to the queen, who had the desire to see us eat, standing behind the door, and we were very well treated after our manner at a small table. Having eaten, the king came again to me to chat, until my men had eaten, meanwhile he fasted until we had departed.

The next day, when I purposed to depart, it rained so hard that I had to remain. Meanwhile I went to view all the *pagoden*[87], which are made not without great art, among which some are five or six fathoms in height, proportioned symmetrically. I imagine that they are made according to the size of Adam, because the length and breadth exactly correspond with the footsteps of Adam, which I also saw and measured, they are 7½ spans long and 3½ broad, they are those whereof Jan Huygen writes[88], which the king caused to be brought from the mountain into the city[89].

The same evening I was again with the king, in order to take leave, who recommended his affairs to me in the strongest manner, and begged me that I would only make

---

86. With the foregoing account of Dom João's defeat of the Portuguese under Pedro Lopes de Sousa, and capture of and marriage with Dona Catharina, compare that given by the Spilbergen diarist, derived probably from the same source (supra,); also that in the description of Ceylon interpolated by de Bry at the end of Bree's diary of de Weert's second visit.

87. De Weert here uses the word *pagode* in the (now obsolete) sense of "idol," whereas the Spilbergen diarist almost invariably uses it with the ordinary meaning of "temple" or "dagaba."

88. See Linschoten i, 79.

89. Cf. the statement of the Spilbergen diarist (supra, B1). DB. has embodied the above paragraph almost verbatim in the description of Ceylon interpolated by him at the end of Bree's diary of de Weert's second visit.

haste, [and] he would meanwhile (if the Portuguese left him in peace) make about 1,000 quintals of cinnamon, which if I came back with help I should have for nothing, or without help for money. He also presented to me in recompense for my presents 25 quintals of cinnamon and 16 quintals of pepper, and for my kitchen, so he said, five quintals of each though I got none or not much, because they were hindered from coming down by the great rain, and on getting aboard I could not wait for them[90]

On the return journey the king sent with me his highest captain (who is a Portuguese[91]) with 50 or [92] 60 men to convoy me and at the same time view my ship; and I was again treated and defrayed[93] as before. He also sent me the first two days food from his house, with wine and some confections[94], so that I was astonished at his munificence[95].

This is what I could not forbear to write at length to your honor, hoping that it will not trouble your honor to peruse the same and consider somewhat over the matter. Were I to describe in particular all the magnificence and treatment of the reception and on the journey, I should be tired of writing. I place this alone before your honor, in order that you may be able to realize what kind of a king and what an island we could have devoted to us with little trouble and great profit,—a king powerful in troops, a brave

90. DS. (and DB.) has instead of this paragraph, the following: "And as the vice-admiral declared that he would assist him with greater force and to that end sail to Achin in order to find there the other ships of his fleet, and to return, the king was agreeable thereto, presenting the vice-admiral with 25 quintals of cinnamon and 16 quintals of pepper."

91. Manuel Dias D.S. (and DB.) omits the words in parenthesis.

92. DS. (and DB.) omits "50 or."

93. The copy has "geadforyeert," which must be an error for "gedefroyeert" (see supra, note 18).

94. DS. (and DB.) has "wine, food, confitures and other delicacies in great abundance." Here the Dutch summary of de Weert's letter ends, and there follow the statements:—"The two ships *Vlissingen* and *der Goes* sailed on 11th. December a°. 1602 from Seylon for Achin. On 14th January, 1603 the ship *Zirckzee* with the vice-admiral sailed from Zeylon for Achin. On 5th February following the ship *Zirckzee* came into the roadstead at Achin, finding there the aforsaid two other ships." (See infra, D2,).

95. The copy has "magnificence." which may be right.

soldier and much inclined towards us, who every day wishes for once to rule in his country over such people as ours, and even to send his son if he were old enough to his excellency in order there to learn good manners and the art of war, a king, I say, who now offers us even his country and means, —a country as fertile as any situated among all the East Indian [countries] that alone yields the cinnamon, which we can now bring into our hands alone, without either Portuguese or Turk[96] being able to obtain a pound thereof, except a little not very good from Nagapatam, and that for nothing, a country as well situated for a place of departure for our ships as any other could be[97], from whence one would be able to direct the trade in East India, as the Portuguese [do] in Goa, to the detriment of the Portuguese, and none more convenient, since we have the king of the country and the people friendly to which also all ships that wish to come from Goa and that quarter to Santhorne, Bengaelen, Pegu, Malacka, Achin, must approach, in order to recognise the land, and so set a fixed course[98], namely, Punta de Galle, which we should have to capture, [and] thereabouts either build or cause to be built a fort, [and] garrison it ourselves[99], I do not know how we should be able to justify not having availed ourselves of such an opportunity, [and] I doubt, not also that if your honor were here in person you would no longer deliberate thereover, the more so, since now at this time we must not neglect anything anywhere, and even in five or six months shall find no pepper.

I greatly regret that we are so badly provided with men against such occurrences, because we shall have to leave there at least fifty men, the which makes my heart bleed,

---

96. The word "Turk" here is evidently used to denominate the Muhammadan traders (Moors) of the East in general.

97. In the earlier part of this letter de Weert, speaking of the want of a safe place whence the Dutch ships could sail to all parts, says: "the which we hope to find in Zeylon, whither we were invited.

98. Compare the statement of D. Francisco de Almeida in his letter of September-December, 1508 to the King of Portugal, as given in C.A.S. Jl. xix 367. See F2, at note 6.

99. The Portuguese already had a fort at Galle, but it was a very poor one (see C.A.S. Jl. xx. 404 note 3.)

so long as we do not yet know where we shall get our lading. Consequently, in case your honor could spare from all your ships fifty men, selecting mostly from those that have first to sail for home, they would be very serviceable to us, the more so, if some among them were somewhat experienced in the art of war : if not, it will not be inexpedient that your honor by the first opportunity recommend this to our masters the directors, so that at least two hundred soldiers may be brought there ; because it were better not to begin than to finish badly. We shall not fail to advise your honor by the first opportunity of the success of our enterprise. so that you may act accordingly[100]

....This first April, 1603 on board ship before Atchijn.

Your honor's obedient servant,

(*Signed*) SEBALT DE WEERT,

Your honor's Vice-admiral.

---

100. Little did the writer think that a sudden and violent death and a nameless grave awaited him in the island on which he had set such hopes ; and that the "success" of the "enterprise" would be disgrace and disaster.

ANNEXURE D.

ACCOUNT OF DE WEERT'S SECOND VISIT TO CEYLON AND MASSACRE, WRITTEN SHORTLY AFTER THE RECEPTION OF THE NEWS IN HOLLAND IN MARCH, 1604[1].

....The 8th March, 1603, there came also to Achin three ships of the same admiralship, named *Hollandia*, *Hollandtschen Tuyn sc Sterre*[2], and the vice-admiral bought there

1. This is taken from one of the "Documents for the History of the Netherlanders in the East," communicated by Mr. P. A. Tiele to the Historical Society of Utracht, and printed in that body's, *Bydragen en Mededeelingen*, 6e deel (1883), pp. 222-376. This document is No. III, and is entitled "Discourse" [*i.e.*, narrative] and advertence [*i.e.*, announcement] of the following ships, [that] sailed from the United Provinces east of the cape *bonae spei*, what kingdoms and countries they visited, how they were received, treated, and what presentations of places, commerces and friendships were made to the admiral, vice-admiral and merchants [and] what new knowledge of trade was obtained by them. All extracted from the papers, letters and advertisements [i.e., announcements,] received the 17th [in orig. "xvii en," but this must be our error: see below] March anno 1604 by the ships the *Eendracht* and *Maecht van Enckhuysen*. [Firstly of the *Haerlem* and *Leyden* under van Neck, than of the *Alckmaer* and *Witten Leeuw* under van Heenskersk]. Finally of the fourteen ships and yacht, over which is admiral Wybrandt Warwyck, whereof three sailed in the year 1602 on 30th March from Zealand, and the rest on 17th and 18th June *anno* aforesaid from the Texel and the Maas." After describing the doings of the ships under van Neck and van Heenskerck, the writer says: "Coming further to the 14 ships and a yacht, "and he then proceeds to give a summary account of de Weert's first visit to Ceylon, taken, as internal evidence proves, from de Weert's own narrative, in his letter of 1st April, 1603, as given above (C1). Then follows this account of de Weert's second visit and massacre, which, though it contains few points of importance that are not related in the fuller narratives of Bree, and Rycks, I here give, as it embodies the earliest information received in Europe of those events. Spilbergen's ships, the *Schaap* and *Lam*, arrived in Holland in company with the *Eendracht* and *Maegt* van *Enckhuysen* on 24th March, 1604, but the writer of this summary does not seem to have had access to the journal of Spilbergen's voyage. The *Hollandsche Tuin* with Bree's very detailed journal did not reach home until December, 1604 or January 1605, and it was not until June, 1607, that the Hollandia, with Jacob Rycks and his diary, returned to Holland. A comparison of this summary, however, with Bree's journal reveals the curious fact that in places the wording is identical (see the references in the following notes). How to explain this I know not, except on the supposition that a copy of the first portion of Bree's journal was sent home by the *Eendracht* or the *Maegt van Rnckhuysen*.

2. See infra, D2, note 21.

of the general Spilberghen a boat of 60 lasts burden [3], so that on 1st April, 1603 he returned again with seven ships from Achin to Seylon, where on the 25th April having come into the road before Batacalou, he sent his letters to Candij to the king, which were handed to his majesty in the leaguer before Mareswalbari [4], who in reply begged that the vice-admiral would come first to Candij and from there to Ventane, in order there to speak with the king, the which (through fear of losing much time) was by the ship's council found not advisable [5], and in the meantime from the 16th to the 21st May, they captured four Portuguese ships, whereof the king having been acquainted with all diligence, he was greatly delighted thereat, informing the vice-admiral that he himself would come to Batacalou in order by word of mouth to discuss everything and to see the captured Portuguese. While on the way to Batacalou the king sent divers messengers and also two letters to the vice-admiral, wherein his majesty among other things desired and begged for the sake of God and his princely excellency not to let the Portuguese[6] go before his arrival, but that they should be delivered over captives or as slaves to him [7]. But the vice-admiral had set free the Portuguese on previous promises and given them a passport signed with his own hand, thinking that he could easily excuse this to the king [8]. The last of May the king arrived near Battecalouwe [9], whither the vice-admiral, the ships' council and two companies of sailors set out on the 1st June to meet his majesty, receiving each other friendly, the vice-admiral requesting that his majesty would be pleased to come in the afternoon to the shore and inspect the ships. Thereupon the king answered that this was inconvenient for him that day, but that next day he would come to the shore and then to the ship, wherefore

---

3. See infra, D2.
4. Sic, for Manicrawari (Manikkadawara). see infra, D2. s.d. 13th May.
5. See infra D2, s.d. 13th May.
6. In orig. "passeren."
7. Cf. infra, D2. s.d. 25th May.
8. See infra, D2, s.d. 28th May.
9. Cf. what follows with the account in Bree's diary infra, s.d. 31st May, et seq.

the vice-admiral (at the command of the king) commanded the most of his men to depart on board ship, wishing to keep by him only one from the council[10], one of the assistants[11], and 6 or 7 musketeers, commanding that the rest should come again to the shore on the following day in like order. Notwithstanding this some of the sailors (contrary to the command) remained here and there in the taverns on land. After the departure of the men, the king and vice-admiral being in debate about coming on board ship, the king answered, "you have required me [to come] from Candi to Ventane; from there at your pleasure I have come 30 miles further to Batacalou, [and] being here you are not yet satisfied, but require me to come to the shore and from the shore on board ship; such a request is to me suspicious." Whereupon the vice-admiral is said to have answered [6]. If the king would not trust him [so far as] to come on board ship, that then he with his ships would leave not for Punta Galle but for home. At which answer the king was so enraged that he commanded the *Modlear*, a Portuguese renegado, to bind the vice-admiral and thereafter to kill him and all other Dutch. From which command the vice-admiral and about 49 men besides were killed. But it is surmised by some persons of the fleet, that this murder did not have its origin in the aforesaid answer; as the king had before that informed the vice-admiral by letters: "If you release the Portuguese, I shall hold you as no friend." The ships remaining there a certain time longer, the inhabitants meanwhile came every day on board under the signal of the white flag[12]. The king of Candi also sent his ambassador Arathes[13] with letters, seeking a renewal of friendship and peace, exculpating himself of the deed done [by asserting it] to have happened through misunderstanding on both sides. But the ships' council did not accept such excuses, and let the matter rest there[14]. From there the ship *der Goes* sailed for Bantam: the three ships *Vlissinghen, de Sterre* and *der*

10. Thomas of Tongerloo? (see Bree, infra, s.d. 1st June).
11. Hendrick Lendgies? (see Bree, infra, s.d. 1st June).
12. Cf. infra, D2, s.d. 20th June.
13. A misreading for "arache" (see infra, D2. s.d. 11th June.)
14. Cf. infra, D2, s.d. 16th June.

Hollandtschen Tuyn for Achin, the remaining three *Zirckzee, Hollandia* and *Het Boot* for Negapatam and along the coast of Choromandel[15]. The other eight ships named *Mauritius, de Sonne, Mane, Nassau, Maecht van Euckhuysen, Eendracht, Erasmus, Rotterdam* and the yacht *het Paepegaeytgen* came before Bantam the 29th April *Anno*, 1603[16]. Likewise also there arrived there from Seylon the 13th August *anno*, 1603 the ship *der Goes*[17]. The aforesaid 9 ships and the yacht were destined and some sailed for divers quarters, to wit: *Erasmus and Nassau* the 6th June, *a*° 1603 for China; *de Maecht van Euckhuysen* and *d'Eendracht* fully laden with spiceries the 29th August, 1603, for Holland, which by the blessing of the Almighty arrived safely; *Mauritius* and *Rotterdam*, having been fully laden with spiceries at Grisse and next at Bantam, were destined for Holland; *de Sonne, Mane, der Goes* and *het Papegayken* were destined for the Moluques and Banda, and [in the event of] not getting their cargo there, for China. May the Almighty Holy God be pleased to guard them together and bring them with prosperity to their fatherland.

ANNEXURE D2.

DIARY OF JAN HARMENSZ BREE.

Jan Harmensz Bree was upper-merchant on board the *Hollantse Tuyn*, one of the three ships detached by van Warwijck from his fleet after passing the Cape, and despatched to Achin to join the three vessels under de Weert. Hence he gives no account of de Weert's first visit to Ceylon; but of the second, and disastrous, expedition he has left a detailed and most valuable description. The original diary kept by Bree to within a short time of his death is no longer extant; but a copy of it seems to have fallen, soon after the return to Holland (at the end of 1604 or beginning of 1605) of the above-named ship, into the hands of the brothers de

15. See infra, D2. s.dd. 11th and 20th June.
16 See infra, D2.
17. See supra, B1, s.d.

Bry of Frankfort, who were then bringing out in parts their famous collection of voyages. Fearing apparently that they might be forestalled by their rival Hulsius [1], the de Brys published in 1605 a slightly abridged translation of Bree's journal, preceded by a translation of the voyage of van Neck (1600-3) [2], in small quarto form [3], under the title of *zwo vuderschiedliche newe Schiffarten, Nemlich, &c.*, and illustrated with eleven plates (all probably imaginary), one of which depicts de Weert's reception by the "king" of Batticaloa and the feats of the juggler, and the other the massacre of de Weert and his companions. On the back of the last page is a note by the publishers, apologizing for the misprints and other errors in this hastily issued preliminary edition. The preface to this edition differs from that of 1606, and, as I have said, portions of Bree's journal are omitted[4] : otherwise, except for slight variations in spelling, and the correction of some misprints and the perpetration of new ones, the matter in the second edition appears to be identical with that of the first [5]. This second edition, issued in 1606, is in folio form, and bears the title *Achter Theil der*

1. In his *Achte Schiffart* (Frankfort, 1605) Hulsius gives a summary of the Holland and Zealand voyages to the East India, from 1599 to 1603. In cap. xviii. (p. 53) he gives the names of the 15 ships that sailed in 1602, but does not even mention de Weert. He says :—" *Zierickzee, Vlissing, Ter Veer* [*sic* !] sailed for the kingdom of Achem. situated in the island of Sumatra," but there is not a word about Ceylon.

2. In this year they also issued in the same form a preliminary edition of their translation of the Spilbergen journal. Of this extremely rare edition there is a copy (wanting the plates) in the Grenville Library of the British Museum.

3. The British Museum possesses two copies of this very rare edition,—one, imperfect, in the Grenville Library, the other, perfect in every particular. (The latter contains a note on the flysheet by the well-known American bibliophil, Mr. Henry Stevans, saying that he had seen only one other copy in that condition). Tiele appears to have been ignorant of this edition and that of Spilbergen mentioned in the previous note : at any ratê he does not mention them in his *Mémoire Bibliographique sur les Journaux des Navigateurs Neerlandais*.

4. The part of Bree's diary omitted covers the entries from 20th June to 15th, July (see below under those dates). The last paragraph of the description of Ceylon interpolated by the edition is also wanting in the first edition.

5. I have compared only the portions of Bree's diary relating to Ceylon : the journal of van Neck's voyage I have not looked at.

Orientalischen Indien, begreiffend....Darvach Ein Historia, so von Johan Herman von Bree, Obersten Hamdelsmann auff dern Schiff der Holländische Zaun genannt, in Gleichmessiger Rayse von An. 1602: *biss in An* 1604. *auffgereichnet worden. Alles auss Niderländischer Verzeichnis in Hochteutscher Sprache beschrieben, Durch M. Gotthardt Artus von Dantzig*[1] .. The translator Artus was a somewhat voluminous writer [2], and was at this time employed by the brothers de Bry in translating for them various Dutch and other voyages into German and Latin. Some of his translations contain ludicrous blunders[3] , but, so far as one can judge in the absence of the original[4] , his rendering of Bree's journal appears to be pretty accurate. The editors of this translation have supplemented Brees' narrative with information from other sources, the most notable addition being, as I have mentioned, already[5] , a translation of the summarized account of de Weert's first visit to Ceylon, as given in the "Discours advertentie," &c. Though not differentiated in any way from the journal proper, it is fairly easy to distinguish these additions and interpolations[6] . In their address "To the Reader" the editors say :—"These two [narratives of voyages] also do not accord badly with the foregoing seventh part of the *Oriental Indies*, accomplished by the admiral Spielbergen, of whom mention is made in these histories also, since they all three treat of almost the same regions and kingdoms, although they did not all succeed equally well in their visits to these. For although the admiral Spilbergen was in great favour with and highly honored by the king of Candy, and the said king also showed the admiral

1. *Eighth part of the Oriental Indies, comprising....Thereafter a History, as noted down by Johan Herman von Bree, chief merchant on the ship called the Holländische Zaun, in the course of the voyage from the year* 1602 *to the year* 1604. *All transcribed from the Dutch record into the German language, by Mr. Gotthardt Artus of Dantzig.*

2. See *Allgemeine Deutsche Biographie* i. (1875) 613, where the writer (Kelchner) says: "A.'s other works, his..translations from the Dutch, &c. (cf. Adelung) are today no longer of value."

3. Specimens of these are given by Tiele (op. cit. passim). see also infra.

4. That this has been lost is greatly to be deplored.

5. Some of these are noted below.

von Neck all friendship and good-will[1], and also received the vice-admiral Sebalt de Weert at first well, yet in the end the said vice-admiral Sebalt de Weert in this last voyage paid for the banquet, and had with his men to bite the dust."

It was perhaps owing to the discreditable circumstances connected with this expedition of de Weert's to Ceylon that no account of it appeared in Dutch until 1644, when, in his valuable collection of voyages entitled *Begin ende Voortgangh van de Vereenigde Nederlandtsche Geoctroyeerde Oost- Indische Compagnie*[2], Isaac Cornelin of Amsterdam printed a translation, from the German of Artus, of Bree's journal, including some of the German editor's additions, but omittings some, and adding several items of information from Dutch sources[3]. This Dutch translation (of a translation[4]) is on the whole fairly accurate, though in some places the translator has misunderstood the German, and here and there he has abbreviated somewhat[5]. An English translation, by Mr. F. H. de Vos of Galle, from this Dutch version, of the portions describing de Weert's two visits to Ceylon appeared in the *Orientalist, iii*, 68-75, 89-95. As, however, this translation does not represent the Dutch version with perfect accuracy, I have thought well to give a fresh translation, as literal as possible, from the old German version of Artus, appending footnotes where they seemed to be required for the better understanding of incidents described and statements made in the journal and the interpolated matter.

---

1. This is a strange blunder. Jacob van Neck never went to Ceylon at all. The writer is evidently confusing the king of Kandy with the king of Achin, who received all the Dutch commanders favourably. (cf. infra.

2. Regarding this collection see Tiele, op. cit. 9-15.

3. As regards these see Tiele, op. cit. 168-9. See also infra.

4. The fact that Commelin, in whose collection many voyages appeared for the first time, had to depend on the German version of Artus for an account of the voyages of van Warwyck and de Weert justifies us in the belief that even then the original ms. of Bree's journal had disappeared.

5. Some of these errors &c. are noted below.

DESCRIPTION OF THE HISTORY AS RECORDED BY JOHANN HERMAN VON BREE[1], A NATIVE OF THE DISTRICT OF LUYK[2], CHIEF MERCHANT ON A SHIP CALLED THE *HOLLÄNDISCHE ZAUN*[3] ON THE JOURNEY TO THE ORIENTAL INDIES, FROM ANNO 1602 TO ANNO 1604, WHEN HE ENDED HIS LIFE[4]

The three ships[5] from Seeland were ordered to sail to the island of Zeylon, and further to Achin situated in Sumatra[6]

....So that with the divine help they[7] arrived on 10th March [1603] in the harbour before Achin. The ships *Hollandia and der Stern*[8] had arrived there two days before the *Holländische Zaun*[9]. They found there besides three ships of their company, that had sailed from Seeland the last of March [1602], about two-and-a-half months before

1. Tiele (op. cit. 168) calls him Jan Harmensz Bree, which it is to be presumed, was his real name.

2. Probably Linksgestel in North Brabant.

3. The *Hollantse Tuyn* (Dutch Garden). Artus everywhere translates the names of the ships into German unless they bore place-names. I have thought it better to retain his forms of the names.

4. Near the end of the diary, under 7th April, 1604, we read :—"But Johann Hermens, who had hitherto noted down this history had fallen into a great illness, from which he eventually died, and because he had little more opportunity and desire to describe his voyage further, and to continue with the history, we will here add the continuation of it from that of the honorable Frantz von Steinhaufler, who took the place of the abovesaid Johann Hermens." Then almost at the close we are told that on the homeward voyage many died of dysentery among whom also Johann Hermanns upper-merchant describer of this history, was one, who died on 1st June in the year 1604.

5. These were, the *Zierikzee*, Sebald de Weert, clerk, afterwards vice-admiral, Govert Jansz, skipper; the *Vlissingen*, Jan de Decker councillor, Laurens Frans van Vlissingen (or, of Flushing) skipper; *Der Goes*, Martin Jelis Spanjaert skipper.

6. They sailed accordingly on 31st March, 1602, the other 12 vessels under Wybrand van Warwÿck not leaving until 17th June.

7. That is the Dutch on board the *Hollantse Tuyn*, on which ship the diarist Bree was.

8. *De Sterre* (the star).

9. These three ships had been detatched from his fleet by van Warwÿck on his arrival at the Cape of Good Hope, and dispatched in advance to Achin to join de Weert's ships, the admiral with the rest of the fleet proceeding to Bantam, where he arrived on 29th April, 1603.

E 2

them, and also two ships of Moucheron's[10]. namely, a small pinnace and a skiff[11], under the gubernation of Jörgen von Spielbergen, who had already been 22 months away from Holland[12]. In addition they found there three or four Turkish[13] ships from the coast of Negapatam, besides a small Portuguese ship, lying in the river. The three ships from Seeland had refreshed in the bay of Antongil[14], and had sailed from there to the island of Zeylon, to a town called Matecalo, because they had learnt that the two ships of Moucheron's had also been there[15]

[16]The vice-admiral Sebald de Weert had gone up from there with six elephants several days' journey, about 40 miles inland, to the city of Candy to the king of the place, to whom for the most part all other kings and princes of this island are subject, where he was then received right nobly after the manner of the country because the king had previously learnt that their people were also enemies of the Portuguese. As indeed the abovementioned Spielbergen had also been there, who had left with the king the portrait of his excellency Count Moritz, besides four persons of his people, and had afterward departed from there in good friendship.

---

10. Balthasar de Moucheron, a leading merchant of Amsterdam (see introduction).

11. These were the *Schaep* and the *Ram* apparently: the *Lain* had been hired by the English on its arrival at Achin (see supra, B1, note 144) and was at this time still in their service.

12. See introduction.

13. See supra, C1, note 99.

14. On the north-east of Madagascar.

15. This is somewhat puzzling, since it is not said whence de Weert's ships obtained this information. It could not have been from letters left by Spilbergen at Antongil Bay, since none of his ships called there (though Guyon Lefort put into St. Augustine's Bay on the south-west of Madagascar). Perhaps it was from letters left at the Cape that de Weert learnt of Spilbergen's intention of going to Matecalo. Or he may very well have learnt of the project before leaving Holland. In any case he could not possibly have ascertained before arriving at Matecalo that Spilbergen had actually been there (cf de Weert's statement in his letter of 1st April, 1603, supra). This is probably a blundering interpolation of de Bry's.

16. I am not sure whether this paragraph is by Bree, or whether it is an interpolation of the editors, written before it was decided to give a detailed account of de Weert's first visit. The latter supposition seems more probable.

[17]This journey of the abovementioned Sebald de Weert will moreover be described more fully, and is in substance shortly as follows:—That he arrived on 28th November. Anno 1603[18] off the island of Zeylon,....

....

[19]The two ships *Vlissingen* and *die Gauss*[20] sailed on 11th December A.n. 1602 from Zeylon for Achin. On 14th January, Anno 1603 the ship *Zirricksee* with the vice-admiral sailed from Zeylon for Achin, and on 5th February arrived in the harbour there before the town, where he found the abovementioned two other ships. On 8th March there arrived there two other ships, and on the 10th following several more of the same company, namely, *Hollandia*, the *Holländische zaun* and *Stern*[21]. Which when they came in there, they were forthwith informed of this great friendship and promise of the king's, namely, how he had offered to present all the fortresses of the Portuguese to the Hollanders, provided they would help his majesty to expel the former therefrom, because he let it be understood openly that his only hope and trust was, to be freed from the Portuguese with the help and assistance of the Hollanders. But because at this time no lading for the ships was to be got, since it was out of the season, the king said that he would not delay or hinder them, but that they should return after some months, and he would deal with them quite honestly and uprightly, nay, what was even more, if they were able to render him a considerable help against the Portuguese, h would allow to fall to their share every product that was to be found there, and ask no payment therefor.

---

17. Here follows the lengthy interpolation by the de Bry's of the account of de Weert's first visit to Ceylon, translated from the Dutch summary of 1604 (see supra, introduction to C1.)

18. Both editions have this error.

19. This paragraph is evidently an interpolation of the editors. The first portion is from the Dutch summary (cf. supra, C1, introduction).

20. This is one ot Artus's absurd blunders, which he repeats throughout. The real name of the ship was *Der Goes*, from the town in Zealand, and had nothing to do with a *goose*. Curiously enough, the Dutch translation in *Begin ende Voortgangh* perpetuates the error.

21. In taking over this sentence from the Dutch summary de Bry or Artus has altered it so that its statements are erroneous (cf. supra, D1, and see note 23 below).

The vice-admiral had at the request of the king left with him two of his men[22], and thus parting in friendship from him, he came to Achin, where also on 10th March arrived the other ships, as mentioned......[23].

[24]The 20th March, as the Hollanders had learnt that they would have little hope of obtaining pepper within six or seven months, they thought well to take their leave of the king in the friendliest manner, and to ascertain actually how much pepper might be available there at that time. So in the afternoon they proceeded to the court, where they seated themselves in their wonted place; but the *sabandar* came to them, asking them what was their desire. Thereupon the vice-admiral gave him to understand how they had resolved to sail with all six ships from there to Zeilon, and therefore desired to know how much pepper might be available there towards the season, in order that they might act accordingly. The *sabandar* said, they might confidently leave at least two ships there, since there was lading enough available for them there. Thereupon answered the vice-admiral, that he had promised and given his word to the king of Zeilon that he would render him help against the Portuguese, and it was therefore necessary that they repaired

22. Apparently another of de Bry's blunders: de Weert in his letter says nothing about leaving any men behind in Ceylon. Probably de Bry was confusing the two left by Spilbergen.

23. The Spilbergen journalist says:—"The 8th ditto [March, 1603] there arrived in the roadstead of Achien three ships from Hollandt, two of them of Amsterdam, namely the ship *Hollandia*, on which the clerk was Melchior de Voghelaer, the other the ship the *Ster*, the clerk claes Symonssz Meebael, the third the *Hollantschen Tuyn* of Enchuysen, the captain on which was Jacob Pieterssz. The aforesaid three ships on coming into the roadstead respectfully struck their flags, and at once [the commanders] went on board the ship *Zierczee*, in order to find the clerk Sebault de Weert, who was not on board, but soon came with our general, pledging one another and bidding one another welcome. The three aforesaid clerks from Hollant brought the confirmation of [the report] that the companies of Hollandt and Zeelant were united, and also showed letters and orders to the effect that Sebault de Weert was made vice-admiral of the ships in East India, over which Heer Wybrant Warwÿck was now admiral. This good order rejoiced everyone, because it was needful that on the three ships of Zeelant a head should be nominated, since there was already there no little unwillingness and jealousy, because in the ships of Zeelant all the three clerks and skippers whom they called captains stood in one grade."

24. Here we return to Bree.

to him with all six ships, in order that they might have their whole force together....

The 31st March[25] the vice-admiral with several others went to the old and the young king, to take their last leave of them, since they had resolved among themselves to set out at the first opportunity, and sail to the island of Zeylon. Once more they were afterwards well received and treated, and the king asked to send some envoys[26] in their ship to the king of Candy, which they were not able to refuse or deny his majesty, and thus they separated in great friendship, and arrived on board ship.....

....

The 3rd April, as they had well supplied their ships with everything, and had also provided them with ballast or stones from the island of Poullo Way, and fresh water from the river, they set sail from there about three hours before daylight with their six ships and the yacht[27]; and also together with them the admiral Spilbergen with his yacht[28]. They laid their course west north-west, and saw when it was day a little ship following them, which brought to the vice-admiral Sebald de Weert the envoy of the king of Achin to the king of Candy. About midday admiral Spilbergen sailed away from their company, and took his course to Bantam, whence he intended to return to Seeland, to whom the Hollanders intrusted their letters to their friends in their fatherland. But they encountered a north wind, and kept themselves by force west north-west, in the direction of the island of Zeylon. The 4th April they saw a little

25. The Spilbergen diarist says that it was on the 30th that Sebalt de Weert, Spilbergen and others went to take leave of the king.

26. Only one envoy was actually sent (see below), but he had a numerous suite.

27. The six ships were, de Weert's three, the *Zierikzee*, *Vlissingene and Der Goes*, and the three from van Warwÿck's fleet, the *Hollantsch Tuyn*, *Hollandia* and *Ster*; while the yacht was the *Sphaera Mundi*. There was a vessel of Moucheron's bearing this name, which Spilbergee came across at Great Corsico Island in August, 1601, and which may have come out later to Achin, though I can find no record of the fact. On 26th or 27th March, 1603, de Weert bought the yacht *Ram* from Spilbergen; and he may have renamed it the *Sphaera Mundi*.

28. See B1, s.d.

ship, which they afterwards recognized to be the ship that had sailed from them the day before, and intended to go to Negapatam with two elephants. They had afterwards from the 5th to the 12th perfectly calm weather, with varying winds.

The 16th April on a Wednesday a general day of fasting and prayer was appointed on all the ships, to implore and pray God the almighty that he would grant his favour and prosperity to this their intended navigation and voyage, so that the same might be accomplished and well ended to the honour of his name, and the extension of his benefits, as also the welfare of the country and its freeing or releasing from the danger of their sworn, declared enemies the Portuguese, who day and night attempted their lives, honour and possessions. They sailed on further once more with calm weather almost until the 21st April, during which time, several of their people on the ships were carried off by death. But on 21st April in the afternoon they got a fresh wind from the south and south-west, and thus sailed west north-west, until 24th April, when very early in the morning they sighted the island of Zeylon, which lay some seven miles from them. Accordingly they sailed forward thus until the evening, when they let fall there anchor in 17 fathoms' depth, about a mile away from the land.

The 25th they again continued their voyage, and when they had sailed some three miles further along the coast, they came to the roadstead of Matecalo and there came to anchor. Forthwith there came in the afternoon to the vice-admiral some boats from the land, which brought some fruits, and displayed a great joy, which they had on account of their arrival.

The 26th very early in the morning the vice-admiral, with some 130 well armed men from all the ships, went on land, where they remained in a little village[29] not far from the sea-shore, until the very great heat had abated a little. They then marched in good order with banners and drums to Matecalo, to greet the king there, and the vice-admiral

29. I am uncertain as regards the identity of this village,—perhaps Karativu.

sat on an elephant. This town of Matecalo is situated some full two miles inland from the sea-shore[30]. When they arrived there they gave the king some presents, who received the Hollanders right well and friendly: he had quite a hundred men, furnished with their arms,—firelocks and spears,—who had to fire off reciprocally, although they did not yet know how to manage the muskets very well. The vice-admiral delivered over to the king a letter that he had written to the king of Candy, to inform the latter of his arrival, which letter he forthwith dispatched.

The inhabitants of the island showed themselves very glad at the arrival of the Hollanders, who were lodged in special houses, and towards evening there were sent to them by the king [things] to eat, namely, rice, fowls, fish and honey[31], after the manner of the country[32]. They of that place have oxen and buffaloes in plenty, but they do not kill and eat them, and also would not sell them to the Hollanders, because they hold it for a great sin to kill these[33]. When then the Hollanders remained the night there, and thought to rest a little, they were so sorely plagued by the mosquitoes, that they could get no rest the whole night through because the inhabitants of that place also, in order that they may remain untroubled by them, must keep up smoke and fire the whole night through at the place where they sleep.

The 27th in the morning the Hollanders again prepared to start, and marched by another road quite a third nearer[34] to their ships. The vice-admiral with some others remained on land, because the king had promised to send every day seven deer on board the ships.

The 29th early in the morning before daylight one Thomas of Tongerloo[35], commander of the yacht, together

30. Rÿcks (see infra) says "a short mile inland."

31. B. V. has "oil" for "honey."

32. Cf. what Rÿcks says.

33. Cf. the statements of Rÿcks, and see further on under 5 and 8 May.

34. B.V. has "quite three miles round."

35. This unsurnamed Thomas was doubtless a native of Tongerloo-lez-Gheel, in the province of Antwerp. He was killed in the general massacre on 1 June (see under that date infra).

with some others, proceeded in the vice-admiral's boat towards the north, some two miles, to a village called Polygamme,[36], to greet the headman of that place with some small presents. This village is situated across a river about an hour's journey from the the shore. At the same time the boat of the *Holländische Zaun* also, together with the boat of the *Vlissingen*, proceeded to the south, to a place called Panane[37], situated some ten miles from there. They also took with them some merchandise and wares, to exchange and barter these at that place as also at other places on the way for fowls and other produce[38].

The 30th April at about midday the king of Matecalo came to the sea-shore with nine or ten elephants and some 200 men, all armed with spears, crossbows, bare swords and firelocks. He himself was clad from above in a pure white, delicate cotton shirt, over which [was] a fine cotton or silk jacket, of gray colour, that was fastened down the front with some little buttons. As further regards him, he was wrapped round the legs and privities with a fine cloth; he had on his head a red cap with a seam that extended from the front to the back part, edged with inferior gold, and having his ears hanging long downwards as far as his shoulders, in which were fixed some small golden rings[39]. The Hollanders on board the ships, when they had learnt that the king was at the shore, to please him they fired on each ship three salvoes, thereupon forthwith the vice-admiral together with some others and a body of musketeers armed with firelocks and muskets went ashore, when they greeted one another, and had a conversation with each other for a long time through an interpreter; and the king said among other

36. Pālukāmam or Pàlugama, a village on the western shore of the lake, about a third of the way up. (See Casie Chitty's *Gaz*). The distance given (say 8 miles) is rather too little. De Jonge (op. cit. iii. 11 in 1, 14), wrongly indentifies "Poligamme" or "Poleigamme" with "Billigamme" (Weligama).

37. In all the other places where this name occurs it is misprinted "Panane." The place meant is Pànawa, on the south-east coast. The distance given (say 40 miles) is nearly right. By land the distance is somewhat longer.

38. Cf. Bree infra, who differs as to which ship's, boats went to Palukàmàm and Pànawa respectively

39. See under the description of Ceylon at the end, note 116.

things that some ten or twelve years before there had been in that place a soothsayer, who had prophesied that within about ten or twelve years a new people would come there, that would expel all the Portuguese from the island: therefore he held it for certain that they the Hollanders must be that new people, since they came as enemies of the Portuguese[40]. He had brought with him for them much fish and some fruit, such as *bonanas, coquos* and the like, besides a deer, and in the evening departed again with his men.

Shortly before his departure the Hollanders experienced a strange adventure with a juggler, who was behung with iron chains, and had besides a square copper plate suspended from his neck, on which the Hollanders could see some figures and likenesses of the devil. He leaped about with great vehemence crying and shouting, so that the Hollanders with astonishment desired to see what would come of it in the end. Thereupon be came rushing up to them, laid aside the copper plate, shouted and cried, and made a great turmoil, after which he took a broad knife, like a bow-spear, that was fasten to a thick iron chain, stuck this into himself through the thick flesh of his thigh above the knee, drew the chain through, and let it thus remain in the wound. Once more he leaped about with great vehemence crying and shouting, and by certain signs gave [them] to understand that he would afterwards stick through his neck a long knife that he had with him, but as the Hollanders had not much pleasure in looking on at this, they went away from him; and it was told them afterwards that he had cleansed with water and washed out the interior of the wound, and had afterwards bound over it a bit of an earthen pot; and the Hollanders had seen many marks on his legs, from which they could infer that he had done this often before.

The 1st May nothing particular happened, only that they bought daily on the shore from those that were appointed thereto fowls, *bonanas, coquos* and other fruits, which were brought thither from the country, and that indeed very

40. On this and other like prophecies see my paper in the *Ceylon National Review* for August, 1908, pp 261-5.

cheap, for some little bits of lead[41], small mirrors, knives, &c. The Hollanders also went daily awalking, some to fish, some to fetch fresh water from the wells that were made on the shore, some hither and thither into the country and in the woods to shoot game and birds, and thus awaited the answer from the king of Candy, having to act in accordance therewith.

The 2nd May the boat came back from Poligamme [with our people], who could not sufficiently extol the exceedingly great friendship that was shown them there by the headman of that place, and with what great joy the inhabitants had received them there. The headman had had them as guests, and had entertained them in his house magnificently with many dishes after the manner of the country, when they sat down on cotton cloths, and the headman himself in his own person served them, and had said that the whole country stood open to them, and that he would be heartily glad if the general would sometime visit him, whom he would come to meet at the shore with his people, and thus receive him. When it was evening he gave the Hollanders some [men] with torches, who conducted them through the wood, and brought them back to the shore, when they thus returned on board ship.

The 3rd May the boats that had gone four days before to Panane returned to the ships. This Panane was situated some ten miles distant from their ships up southward, a good bit of a way inland from the sea-shore, where they were then also very well received by the king or chief, who had shown them all friendship. They brought some fowls, *bonanas, coquos*, and other fruits, and had also on the way lain at a village on the shore called Tirecoy[42]; they brought also a little rice with them, that they had exchanged and bartered for lead[43], small mirrors, knives and the like.

The 4th May the vice-admiral together with some others went left in two boats for Poligamme, to visit and greet the king of that place, according to his wish. About mid-

41. B.V. has "tin."
42. Tirukkóvil, on which see infra, note 101.
43. B.V. again has "tin."

day they saw a ship sailing southwards of them, wherefore in great haste they equipped a boat with men, and sent it after the ship. But it was a barque laden with rice, on which were some blacks or moors, who had sailed from there twenty days before, they could not well understand whither they intended, but gave them the impression that they were minded to sail somewhere towards the Punto di Gallo. A few days before the lightning had killed a man on the abovesaid barque and thrown another to the ground, without causing them further injury.

The 5th both boats returned from Poligamme, where they were well received by the king[44], but yet not with such prodigality as had certainly been intimated to them and they had been given to understand. But as the Hollanders could not obtain enough refreshment and food to their liking, and the king of Matecalo did not do justice to his promise, since he had promised that he would have delivered to them every day at the shore seven deer (although he had not, save that he had sent them some deer and wild boar), therefore some of the Hollanders went into the forest with their firelocks and there shot some small oxen, in order afterwards to divide them out among the ships. When the inhabitants learnt of this they were very dissatisfied therewith, and brought a great complaint about this loss and molestation: It is true that the vice-admiral went next day himself on shore, in order to pacify them, as best he could, since their intention was not other than to pay them for them, and to well satisfy everybody, or to pacify them on that account. And they impressed upon them this consideration or thought, that, because they refused to sell these to them, they were obliged themselves to see to it how they could come by them, and afterwards pay them for them; but they judged the matter for otherwise.

The 8th instant the Hollanders again went out to shoot oxen, but the inhabitants were greatly enraged thereat, cried out and took it in very bad part. Consequently some of the Hollanders went to Matecalo to speak to the king

---

44. *Cf.* Rycks infra.

about this and to intreat him, that he would pacify the persons to whom the oxen belonged on that account, since they wished to pay for those oxen. But the king took it in equally bad part, and said, that they had truly come there as friends, but now showed themselves in deed far otherwise, because the Portuguese also had never acted so, wherefore he had liefer lose his life then than he should suffer and permit that any longer. There were also some persons who then said that the souls of the oxen that were thus killed went forthwith down into hell, which were a very pitiable matter. At last the king said, in case they abstained therefrom, and would no more act so, it would be forgiven them, and further he would daily supply the ships with rice and other things needed, as much as was possible to him.[45]

The 12th there came to the vice-admiral, the captain or commander of the little ship or *champan*, as they call it there[46], that the Hollanders had found there, and that was now mostly laden with rice, with the intention of sailing from there at the first opportunity, and to take its course to a place situated in the north of the same island, called Jaffnapatam. He brought with him four fowls and some fruits, which he presented to the vice-admiral, begging the latter at the same time that he would give and let him have a passport, so that he might sail the sea safely as regarded the Hollanders, which was at once granted to him.

The 13th following there arrived at Matecaio five persons[47] from Candy, three of whom came on the following day to the shore, and so further on board ship to the vice-admiral. They brought with them a letter, that was dated the 9th instant, from one called Erasmus Matsberger, who was a German, and had been left at Candy by General Spil-

45. On the above cf. what Rÿcks says, infrà, s.d. 6 May.

46. The Chinese word *sanpan* (see *Hobson-Jobson s.v.* "sampan") has become naturalized in Sinhalese under the form *hambána*, "a large boat, Malabar vessel, dhoney" (Clough), having apparently come through the Tamil *sampân*. It forms the first component of the place-names Hambantota and Sammanturei.

47. Rycks (infra, s.d. 14th May) says two Dutchmen." (Cf below under 18th May).

bergen, but is now in the service of the united company[48] This was an answer to the letter that the vice-admiral had sent to the king of Candy. The king, however, was in the camp at Manicrawari, to complete his former triumph and victory[49], on which account the answer had been so long in coming. The Hollanders learnt further from this letter of the abovementioned Matsberger's the good affection and inclination of the king's, which he once again bore towards their nation ; likewise also the joy and great satisfaction that he had at their arrival : he accordingly asked further that at the earliest opportunity they would proceed with their ships to the fortress of Punto de Gallo, because he would besiege it by land ; with the promise, that all that he had promised his son (so he called the vice-admiral) should be observed to him, and if he were to capture the fortress of Punto de Gallo, he would deliver yearly on board the Dutch ships 1,000 quintals of cinnamon and 1,000 quintals of pepper. The abovementioned Matsberger in his letter also further confirmed and ratified that up to then he had discovered not the least falsehood or deception in the king.

So it was accordingly resolved, that at the earliest opportunity they should sail with all seven ships for the abovementioned fortress of Punto de Gallo. It is true that the king had desired the vice-admiral to come at the earliest opportunity to a place called Vintana, that is situated between Matecalo and Candy, whither he would come to meet him, to have a conversation with him on all matters ; but in order that they might lose no time, it was thought well to intermit that, which was then at once made known to the king, with the intimation that he would at the very soonest opportunity come and beleaguer the abovementioned fortress with some two or three thousand men, wherefore the Hollanders would also use diligence that they might also come thither with their ships at the earliest opportunity, and besiege it by sea.

---

48. The United East India Company having been formed subsequent to Spilbergen's departure for the East (see introduction).

49. Unfortunately we have no details of these events, there being a lacuna in the Portuguese history for this period.

The 16th May very early in the morning they saw a ship sailing to the roadstead some two miles distant from them southwards: consequently they forthwith sent three boats towards her, and about midday they also dispatched three of their ships, namely, the *Hollandia*, the *Holländische Zaun* and the *Stern*, towards her. When however the boats came up [to her] they saw that she was a big Portuguese ship, wherefore one boat, that of the *Holländische Zaun*, immediately sailed back to bring the vice-admiral the tidings thereof, but the other two boats sailed on to speak to the Portuguese that they should strike their sail and surrender. Thereupon they immediately fired upon the boats with firelocks and muskets, whereby a man was killed, so that they sheered off again, and kept between the ship and the land, during which time a yacht well equipped with men was in addition dispatched by the vice-admiral. When then this [yacht] came up [to her], and the Portuguese saw the three abovementioned ships also sailing up behind her, they let their sail fall, and forthwith dispatched some among them to the Hollanders, begging for mercy, and that only their lives might be spared to them, which was then promised and assured to them. Thereupon the captain of the ship, named Lopo Alvares, together with a merchant, was sent to the vice-admiral, who at once ordered the ship to be taken possession of and manned with a prize-crew. This ship was a large one, of some 200 lasts, named *Nostra Senora de Rosario*,[50] and had sailed from Cochin some six days before; she intended to voyage to Negopatan, and from there on to Bengala; she had [on board] some twenty Portuguese and blacks or Moors, besides many women. In the evening they brought this ship to the harbour alongside of the others of the Hollanders, who had learnt that three other ships as well had been fitted out to sail from Cochin for Negopatan at the earliest opportunity[51].

The 17th May they saw once more early in the morning a ship sailing along the coast to the south of them, towards

50. Correctly, *Nossa Senhora do Rosario*.

51. Cf. Rÿcks infra, s.d.

which five ships[52] and three yachts or[53] boats at once set sail, so that the vice-admiral was left in the harbour alongside of the captured Portuguese ship with only a yacht. They could not reach the ship however the whole day. And then in the evening a gale sprang up, so that the ships could not keep together, or preserve any order.

The 18th early in the morning three ships were still together, namely, the *Hollandia*, the *Holländische Zaun* and the *Stern*, which came back in the evening into the harbour to the vice-admiral, when they learnt the tidings that two Dutchmen had come with letters from Candy and the king. Soon afterwards the vice-admiral's boat also came into harbour, which with the help of the ship *Vlissingen* had captured the same day another ship, but not the same that we have mentioned before, named *Madre de Dios*, also of 200 lasts' burden, in which however there was nothing. They brought with them the clerk of the latter, because the captain was already previously with the vice-admiral, for it also came from Cochin, and intended to sail to Negopatan.

The 19th instant early in the morning they saw once more a strange ship, towards which the ship *Hollandia* and the *Stern* with two boats immediately set sail. When they reached this ship she at once surrendered, and they consequently brought her with them in the afternoon into the harbour. She was also from Cochin, and intended to sail for Negopatan, and thence for Malacca, and on to the Philippine Islands. She was of some 70 lasts' burden, named *Sanct Antonio*, and her captain was called Pedro Dassovedo[54]. the same day there came to the vice-admiral the *Modeliar* of Candy, from whom they learnt of the capture of the tortress of Maniarawari and other victories of the king's[55]. Soon after midday the ship named the *Holländische Zaun* with a yacht or[56] boat was dispatched by the vice-admiral

52. Rÿcks (infra, s.d.) names these.

53. These two words should come out. The Dutch had only one yacht in their fleet.

54. Correctly, Pedro de Azevedo.

55. See supra, note 50.

56. Again these two words should come out (see note 54 supra). Rÿcks (infra, s.d.) has "two sloops."

to sail to the north of the roadstead, because they had learnt that one ship was still missing, which they supposed to be the same that has been sighted on the 17th, towards which they had indeed sailed, but had not been able to overtake her; it was presumed however that she must have gone to some part of the district of Trinque de Malo[57], consequently the *Holländische Zaun* was to sail towards Trinque de Malo, and there wait twenty-four hours for her, and if by them she had not been able to learn anything regarding her, she was to return again.

The 20th early in the morning they saw their two ships, namely *Vlissingen* and *die Ganss*[58], coming in, and bringing with them the captured ship *Madre de Dios*, which arrived in harbour in the afternoon. The ship named the *Holländische Zaun*, which had sailed away the previous day, then sighted a ship, which she chased the whole day and throughout the night.

And when on the 21st they came up with her, they captured her without any resistance, but learnt that the day before the captain, skipper and pilot, together with other Portuguese to the number of twenty, had set off in a boat and sailed away from her, so that only a single Portuguese soldier remained on board, besides some blacks or moors; and the ship was also named *Sanct Antonius*.

The 23rd following the ship named the *Holländische Zaun* came into harbour to the other ships there with the captured Portuguese ship[59]; and the latter was of some seventy or eighty lasts, and had on board two very valuable Persian horses. The Hollanders meanwhile received daily letters from the king of Candy, in which the continuance of his victory and conquest was confirmed.

The abovementioned two horses had been bought for 1590 reals of sight, or rixdollars, for they were worth that much, and were also to have been sent to Negopatan. As regards the goods however that were on all four ships, these were nothing special, although the great roomage should

57. Read "Trinquelemale."
58. Cf. "*Der Goes*" (see supra, note 20).
59. Read Rycks infra, s.d.

certainly have required a large [amount of] merchandise They had some sackfuls of wheat, which was very fine, and had come trom Cambayen, also some bell-metal China-roots, some cases of rose-water, and about three iasts of pepper.

The chief reason however why they had captured and taken possession of these ships was the great persecution, molestation and enmity of the Portuguese, which they bear towards the Hollanders, and then, that they wished to satisfy the king of Candy, and show that they were enemies ot the Portuguese, although this turned out more to their hurt than to their advantage.

Now when the tidings of the capture of these ships reached the king of Candy he became very glad and joyous, and on 25th May he got ready to journey towards Matecalo, after that he had previously written to the vice-admiral, and begged on account of his princely excellency and for God's sake not to release the Portuguese, but either to kill them, or to deliver them into his hands.

The 28th they received at the shore some fowls, butter, rice, eggs and fruit, that had been sent to them by the king of Candy.

The 29th however, in accordance with what had at first been granted and promised to the Portuguese at their request to release them, together with a ship in which they could get to Negopatan, this was fulfilled to them, and they were released, with two ships, *Nostra Senora de Rosario* and *Sancto Antonio*[60], on board which all the people were placed, except some slaves, and these desired of their own free will to remain with them. And so these two ships set sail the same day for Negopatan with passports from the vice-admiral, returning thanks very warmly for the great favour and good treatment that had been shown to them the whole time. The Hollanders, it is true, were at first indeed of the opinion that perhaps they might obtain from these ships an experienced steersmen or pilot, who might for a time serve them on the coast of Gallo and Colombo, as also in the bay and on the

60. What became of the other two ships (regarding which Bree is strangely silent) Rÿcks tells us.

coast of Choromandel; but because they begged and prayed so earnestly to release them, they were also allowed to sail. The Hollanders well thought that this freeing and releasing of the Portuguese would not altogether please the king of Candy; but because it had been promised them at first, they had to keep their promise, because moreover it would be unfriendly to kill people that were at that time prisoners, and thereby satisfy the desire of the king.

The 30th May they received tidings that the king of Candy would arrive at Matecalo the following day, wherefore the Hollanders made great preparations to go to meet his majesty and receive him.

The 31st there came to the ships another Dutchman, who had left the king the day before, five miles on that side of Matecalo, so that they could not but think that he would arrive at Matecalo in the evening. They received also the same day some various fruits from the king, which he had sent there before him. Thus on all the ships they got ready to go to meet his majesty the following day, and to receive him with all friendship and honour, to which end therefore a large tent was erected by them on the shore, which they fitted out very handsomely[61], to receive his majesty therein, and from there further, so far as that might please his Majesty, to bring him on board the ship to view them [sic] and afterwards to discuss in good faith everything that might conduce to the utility and the advantage of this voyage and of the country

The 1st June early in the morning the Hollanders from all the ships well armed, together with the vice-admiral and other officers, went ashore, to the number of some 200 men, among them all the drummers, with four drums and two banners[62] When they came on land, they marched thus in good order to meet the king, because the latter had, it is true, not yet arrived at Matecalo, but nevertheless was also not far from there. Consequently then the vice-admiral

61. B.V. very oddly mistranslates these clauses "also fitted out a *chaloupe* [sloop] magnificiently."

62. Compare what follows with the account given by Rÿcks (infra, s.d.)

thought it advisable to proceed somewhat further, and so they went on for about half-a-mile further, when they met the king, who had with him some 300 men, besides some elephants. There they received each other well, and afterwards marched together to Matecalo. Then the envoy from Achin delivered to the king his letter, together with a golden *crys* or dagger[63]. Now after the vice-admiral had spoken with the king a little, he [the king] requested that the Hollanders should all betake themselves back to the shore and on board ship, and return the following day in good time, in the same order and fashion. That they would then together march to the shore, but he desired that the vice-admiral should stay over the right with him with some of his men, which therefore was so done.

As therefore the vice-admiral apprehended no treachery or anything evil, he remained with the king together with some of the chief officials, such as namely, Thomas of Tongerloo[64], Heinrich Lendgies[65], and some others[66]. The men however went back again to the shore, but altogether scattered, and without any order, one in front, another behind, so that the greater part reached the shore, who therefore saved and preserved their lives, because the hindmost were all attacked of a sudden and murdered, although some nevertheless escaped, but some fell down and lay for dead, who were afterwards brought on board ships in a very pitiable condition[67].

The Hollanders on the ships, when they became aware of this sudden attack and murder of their people, knew not what to think, and could not believe that this had happened through or been ordered by the king of Candy, but imagined that it must somehow have happened through a misunderstanding: they had therefore a great desire to learn how matters stood with the vice-admiral and his companions.

63. This is the first mention of the Achin envoy since the notification of his coming on board ships on 3 April, and it is evident that he had not previously met the king of Kandy.

64. See note 36 supra.

65. I cannot find what position this man held.

66. Rÿcks says 25 in all.

67. See under 3 June, et seq.

and on that account very early the next day sent a youth born in the island on shore with a letter, because they were still in good hope of the vice-admiral and his companions; the boat of the *Holländische Zaun* also went to land in case of getting any tidings of how the affair came about. Meanwhile however came the envoy from Achin, together with two of his company, who had a flag of truce and a letter, which he showed from afar to the Hollanders, who at once went to him in a boat, and received the letter, which was written in the Portuguese language in the name of the king of Candy[68], from which then the Hollanders learnt that the vice-admiral with all his people had perished. The cause of this this king wished to lay entirely on the vice-admiral, who had wanted by force to compel and inveigle the king on to the ship. He consequently announced that if the Hollanders desired henceforth to have with him his friendship and peace he would be pleased, but in case they did not desire this, but wished to have war, it was not of much consequence to him, they might do as they liked; but they must write an answer in the Portuguese language, for the reason that no one remained or was available that could read their language. These were extremely sad tidings for the Hollanders, and they were sore grieved to hear such a thing of their good friends and brothers.

The envoy from Achin could not say how it stood with the Hollanders, whether they were still living or dead, but said that he himself had fled and had kept himself hidden in the jungle. Others related this in the following manner: that when the vice-admiral had come to the king he had in a friendly way begged or requested that his majesty would be pleased, after the midday meal had been held, to come to the shore and view the ships. Thereupon the king had answered that he was not pleased to do it that day, but that on the following day he would come to the shore and moreover on board the ships: wherefore he requested that the vice-admiral should let his men withdraw, which he had

68. Cf. what is related infra, s.d. 3 June. See also Rycks, infra, s.d.

then done, at the king's request, as apprehending no evil, and had ordered his men to betake themselves on board ship, excepting some commanders and officials and ship's councillors, together with six or seven musketeers. He had however bidden his men to retire to the shore in the same order in which they had come, who however in disregard of this retired in complete disorder, and partly remained going in and out of the taverns of the town. After the men had withdrawn, and the vice-admiral had got into conversation with the king, and further had begged his majesty to come on board the ships, he had answered: "At first you asked that I should come from Candy to Vintana, whence also to please you I travelled full thirty miles hither to Matecalo.' But now that I have come hither, you are not yet content, but require me first at the shore, and [then] on the ship: this request of yours is not a little suspicious to me." To which then the admiral had replied: that in case the king did not trust him so as to come on board ship, then he also would not go with his ships to Punto de Gallo, but take his way back to whence he came: at which reply the king was so enraged, that he forthwith commanded the *modeliar*, who was a Portuguese by birth[69], to bind the vice-admiral, and afterwards to kill him with all his companions. Through which command then the vice-admiral with 49 men besides was murdered and killed[70]. There are however many of this opinion, that this murder and homicide had its cause and origin not in the answer of the vice-admiral, but in this, that he had not fulfilled the command of the king, since he had often bidden and written to him, that in case he should release the Portuguese, he should neither hold nor acknowledge him as a friend[71].

The king's letter, which he had done in the Portuguese language, began in this way: "God yesterday executed right and justice, and this for reasons." To this letter the Hollanders immediately on 2 June replied to the king

---

69. Manuel Dias (see supra, B1, note 51).
70. According to Rÿcks, 47 were killed.
71. Bree, it will be noticed, says nothing of de Weerts' being intoxicated, as Rÿcks and Antonio Martins tell us he was.

in writing, and entrusted the letter to a Portuguese woman, who had formerly been a slave in Candy, and had been set free by the vice-admiral. This woman, when she came to Matecalo, and there learnt that the Hollanders were all killed, and that the king with his men had set off again early in the morning, forthwith sent a man with the letter after the king, who overtook him on the way, and delivered the letter to him, and also at once got a reply from him, which began as follows : " God does justice to those that ask justice of him, and that deserve it from him."[72]

The 3rd June the boat of the ship called the *Holländische Zaun* went to the land, in case anyone of the Hollanders were alive, to render him help, when they saw sitting on the shore quite naked and bare one of their [men], whom they took into the boat. This was a boatswain of the ship *Vlissingen*; he had his body full of wounds, and had thus wounded lain for dead two whole nights long in the first village, whence he was then carried out quite naked : he said, that very early that morning two men had come out of the village, who had lifted him up in a mat, and had brought him to the shore, whence they had immediately run away, so that they might not be recognized. At the same time another boatswain was recovered, who though sore wounded had betaken himself from the land into the water, and had afterwards remained in the jungle. In the evening came three more persons of the company of the envoy from Achin, as also the abovementioned woman, who brought a letter from the king, from which the Hollanders learnt the lamentable and pitiful tragedy of the murder of the vice-admiral with his companions, up to some 50 persons, the cause of which the king laid solely and alone on the vice-admiral, in that, after he had journeyed 30 miles from Candy to Matecalo, there to speak with the vice-admiral on all things, he would have had him by force to the shore and from there on board ship, which treachery however God had not been willing to allow or permit ; he also referred to the captured ships and

72. Cf. the quotations from the king's letters given above with those given by Baldacus, infra, F5.

Portuguese prisoners, who, he thought, would have been sent ashore, but whom they had allowed to go away again free and unhindred all together in two ships, which was not proper in his friends, and in case they still desired his friendship and peace, such should be acceptable and pleassing to him, but if not, as they wished, so also would he[73].

This misfortune then, that had so suddenly overtaken the Hollanders, they found hard to brook, owing to the loss of so many men, and that now was taken from them all hope of accomplishing anything useful in the island. Because however they were now sufficiently assured of the death of the vice-admiral, on 4 June Jacob Petersen of Enckhausen was chosen in the place of the abovementioned as a vice-admiral, and was transferred from the Enckhausie ship to the ship *Zirricksee*[74]. In the evening they brought another badly wounded [man] from the shore on board ship, and on the 5th following the envoy from Achin together with three other Achinese came on board the vice-admiral's ship.

The 6th June following the king of Matecalo asked that some Hollanders would come to him, to speak with him, wherefore at noon a boat went to land, which took in the two[75] men of the king's as hostages and in exchange put ashore two others, who went to Matecalo, and took with them their spades or shovels, to bury the dead bodies of the Hollanders that lay strewn here and there on the land.

The 7th instant these two men came back again from the king of Matecalo to the shore, and gave a signal to fetch them back, whereupon the boat was got ready with the hostages[76], who went back to Matecalo. The Hollanders, when they came on board ship, together with one more of the company of him of Achin, related that the king of Matecalo had strongly exculpated himself from all that the king

---

73. This seems to be a repetition of the contents of the letter already mentioned as brought by the Achin envoy.

74. Cf. Rycks s.d. The ship of Enkhuisen was the *Hollantse Tuyn*. Pietersz did not enjoy his new rank for long, since he died on the homeward voyage in the Bay of St. Braz on 19th September 1604, and was buried on shore.

75. B. V. has "three."

76. B. V. inserts "three" before "hostages."

of Candy had done, for which he was heartily sorry, but that it had been carried out by the people of the king of Candy alone, in which of course he had no guilt. He consequently begged quite friendly that the Hollanders would not on that account show any enmity to him and his people, with the offer of his good favour, affection and willingness according to all his power. This apology the Hollanders took in good part, it is true, but nevertheless did not believe everything pending further intelligence.

Then when on 9th June they learnt that yet another of their [men] was at Matecalo severely wounded, they sent a man to the king with some gifts to present to the latter, and to bring the wounded [man] on board ship, when one from Matecalo meanwhile remained as a hostage on the ship. He came back however on 11th June on board ship with the wounded [man] and one more of the company of the Achinese envoy; there was also with him besides one that they call *árache*, which signifies as much as a captain, who brought with him a ring of inferior gold, in which were set some small stones, which the king presented to the vice-admiral.

Meanwhile the Hollanders held a consultation, and thought well that the ship named *die Gauss* should go to Bantam, to warn the ships that were there, to inform them of this misfortune, and to admonish them to seek their lading there. The two ships the *Stern* and *Vlissingen* should go to Achin, to load there as early as possible, and the ship named the *Holländische Zaun* should go with these two, for their greater defence or protection against one named Andreas Furtado, of whom they heard that with the *moison*[77] he wished to come from Malacca before Achin[78]. The vice-admiral however, namely the *Einigkeit*[79], item *Hollandia* and the yacht should sail for Negopatan, and further to Bengala, as should at some time or other be most suitable[80].

77. That is, monsoon (see *Hob.-Job.* s.v.).

78. This was an unfounded rumour regarding Dom André Furtado de Mendoca see Gray's Pyrard, ii 267 n. 3.

79. B. V., copying this extraordinary blunder, has "den *Eendracht*." The *Eendracht*, which was one of the ships of van Warwÿck's fleet did not come to Ceylon at all. The vessel meant is the *Zierikzee*.

80. These arrangements were altered on the 20th and on 13th July (see under those dates).

The 13th June the king of Matecalo sent on board the ships three pigs and a deer.

The 14th an *arache* came to the vice-admiral with an old man as well who could also speak Portuguese, besides yet another of the Achinese envoy's company. And the king sent by these some fowls and civet-balls[81], who went back to land the same day, and on the 15th instant the *arache* again brought a deer on board ship.

The following day, which was the 16th June[82], a Dutchman from Candy with an envoy and letter came on board ship, from the king, who was very apologetic, and desired anew the Hollanders' friendship, and accordingly swore by his god, his soul and children that they should give him credit, and send a man to him to Candy to speak with him, who should then also obtain a sight of the cinnamon and pepper that was there, with the notification that in so far as the Hollanders would still render him assistance, and help to capture the fortresses of Gallo and Colombo, he would fulfil in every way his engagement and promise, and render a complete satisfaction.

In consideration of this they did not think it advisable therefore to leave this island and abandon it, although they had little hope of accomplishing anything useful at this time, yet, in order that they might endeavour the utmost, they considered it well to dispatch to Candy a young fellow named Jacob Cornelisz, who was an under merchant on the ship called the *Holländische Zaun*, with an instruction and a letter to the king of the following contents, namely, that all the cinnamon and pepper that the king might have should be delivered to them at the shore, along with some officials set over and appointed for it, with whom they might actually deal; and they would accordingly pay cash down for all that they should bring them, either in gold or silver, or in other wares and merchandise : in that case they would accept his friendship. As regarded the fortresses of Colombo and

81. Doubtless some preparation of musk from the genette (cf. Tennant's *Nat. Hist. of Ceylon*, 32)

82. According to Rÿcks, this Dutchman arrived on the 17th.

Gallo however, they had in part dispatched their ships[83], to inform their admiral and other ships that were here and there in India of all that had occurred. Such might yet well take place with the earliest opportunity of the *moison*, since they still had to expect daily more ships from their country, when it would not be difficult for them to deliver the abovementioned fortresses into the hands of his majesty.

[84]The 17th there arrived there a ship, laden for the most part with *arecca*; it was from Bellingam, that lies four miles to the north of the Punto di Gallo[85], and intended to go to Negopatan, wherefore the Hollanders put on board the ship some Moors whom they had got from the Portuguese ships, and who wished to go to Negopatan. But because she lay quite close to the shore, the king of Matecalo had the sail taken away from her, and the shipman or captain imprisoned, on account of a yet unpaid debt, which however did not amount to much. There then the aforesaid Moors for the most part came back on to the ships of the Hollanders, but however after a few days the ship set sail, and went on her way.

The 19th instant early in the morning the abovementioned young fellow Jacob Cornelisz as well as the other Dutchman that had come from Candy was dispatched to Matecalo, and further to journey to Candy, and that indeed in the company of the aforesaid envoy from Candy, as also in that of the envoy from Achin and his company, who likewise went with them, to ask for his dismissal. There came however at that time at noon yet two others from Candy to the Hollanders on board ship, who once more persisted strongly that they would send a man to the king and these last two letters were signed by the king himself with some very strange characters and letters, as moreover was his custom to sign such[86]

---

83. This statement in anticipatory.

84. Apparently through an oversight., B. V. omits this paragraph.

85. For "north" read "south-east," and the distance named (say 16 miles) is about right.

86. The letters were doubtless subscribed with the royal sign-manual ශ්‍රී.

The 20th they received a letter from the abovementioned Jacob Cornelisz, from Matecalo, in which he announced that only the following day would they set out to make the journey to Candy.

In the evening the two ships the *Stern* and *Vlissingen* set sail for Achin[87], and the ship called *die Gass* [*sic*] left for Bantam[88] ; as regards the remaining three ships however, their voyage was annulled owing to the letter and request of the king of Candy, and a new resolution come to, that the ships *Zirricksee, Hollandia* and the *Hollandische Zaun* together with the yacht should stay there until they learnt what sort of a hope they might have as regards their lading, especially also because the envoy from Achin hoped to receive his dismissal at the very earliest moment, and to repair back to them, that he might then sail back and reach home in one of the ships of the Hollanders[89]. The Hollanders however daily took in fresh water on to the ships, and went well armed in their boats to the shore, there to barter for fowls, eggs, *bonanes*, *coquos*, and other things, which were brought thither in great plenty, now more than before, and they could get them for quite a trifle, such as lead, small mirrors and knives[90]. They kept however as near as ever they could to the land in the boat, to supply their men that went on land with their muskets and pieces of ordnance, because on both sides there was little trust. Thus throughout the four following days the boats brought much from the land, and they supplied themselves to a tolerable extent with provisions. They received also on the 28th from the king of Matecalo once more a deer. On the 29th there were again many people at the shore with a great abundance of fowls and all kinds of fruits, but the Hollanders could

87. Cf. supra, D1.

88. The arrival of this ship, the *Der Goes*, at Bantam on 13 August, 1603, with the news of the massacre is recorded by the Spilbergen diarist (see supra, B1 at end).

89. In the first German edition of Bree's journal all that here follows, down to the end of the entry for 19 July, is omitted, the editor substituting the words : "After they had delayed there however until 20 July they saw on the shore."

90. Cf. Rÿcks s.dd. 27 June to 13 July. For "quite a trifle" B. V. substitutes "Nuremberg-gewgaws."

not get to land owing to the boisterous waves of the sea, and so they had to return with business uneffectuated.

The 7th July there came an *arache* from Matecalo to the vice-admiral asking for a passport for two *champons* or ships that wished to come from Bellingam to the Hollanders, laden with cinnamon and pepper, to sell the latter to the Hollanders there, a little of which he brought with him as a sample: the Hollanders gave him a passport in the Portuguese language, and he returned to land with it.

The 8th there came three more persons to the vice-admiral with some fowls and *coquos* as a present, who said that three Dutch ships were reported to be lying before Jaffnapatam, since one among them had come from there by land, and as they had a *champan* or ship lying in the river of Poligamme, with which they wished to go to Jaffnapatam, they asked for a passport or permit, in order when they came there, that they might not be harmed by those ships. The Hollanders could not well believe that some of their ships should be there, but they made as if they believed it, and accordingly asked if perchance anyone amongst them would go in a ship that they would dispatch thither: they would recompense him for it, and let a permit follow them immediately for their *champan* or ship. They accepted this, it is true, but said however that they must first let the king of Matecalo know of it, and so would return the following day, and one of them should then remain on board the ship to go thither with the Hollanders. But they forgot wholly and entirely their promise and the coming back.

The 9th July they were told of five *champans* or ships that were said to be lying in the river of Poligamme, two of which were laden with elephants, one with ivory, and one with *arecca*; the fifth however had still to load. This again the Hollanders could not believe, namely, that so many *champans* should be lying there, although indeed they had heard before this that the king of Candy was wont to send yearly as a present to some kings on the coast of Choromandel some *champans* with elephants therefore they resolved to send the yacht *Sphe a Mundi* with the long boat of the *Hollandische Zaun* to the place, to fetch the *champans* or ships. so far as any of these were to be found in the river, in order that thus their people might the better and sooner be dispatched from Candy. In the evening however they saw a *champan* or ship coming from the south, wherefore they sent off to it the boat of the vice-admiral, to bring it into the harbour beside their ships.

When they came thither and had cast anchor, the vice-admiral caused the chief men on her to be brought before him, who showed their permit. which had been given to the *arache* on the 7th instant, and said that they had come from Mattone[91], which lay five miles north of the Punto di Gallo and one mile's journey from Bellingham[92]: they had some 8,000 pounds of cinnamon as cargo, which the *Panico mudeliar* (so they called the chief of that place)[93] had sent thither for sale, although he was not so much concerned about its sale (since it was very little) as to know and understand what manner of ships and people they were, as he wished to have friendship with them, wherefore also he exonerated himself from what had taken place through the king of Candy, namely, that he had had no cognisance thereof.

They said further that the *panïco mudeliar* had under him and in his territory six or seven thousand men, all of whom did not much concern themselves about the king of Candy: therefore if the Hollanders would proceed with their ships before the fortress of Punto de Gallo, to besiege the latter, the *panico mudeliar* would march before it by land; and because there were not more than thirty Portuguese present in the fortress[94], they would easily capture and conconquer it without the king of Candy's previous knowledge. The Hollanders however could not believe this, but imagined that it had been thus put forward by the king of Candy.

---

91. An error for "Mattore." After this word B. V. has inserted erroneously "Bellingam"

92. Here again for "north" read "south-east." The distances are understated.

93. This was probably Samarakón Mudaliyár (Dom Fernando) regarding whom see *M. Lit. Reg.* iv. 165.

94. Writing a few years later, the Spanish captain Antonio Martins stated that there were 50 men in garrison in Gale, of which he speaks most contemptuously (see *M. Lit. Reg.* iv. 165).

The cinnamon they bought of them, received, and paid for and they afterwards went to land with the *champan*, and drew it up high and dry, because they had announced that they would go to Matore by land: they would have liked to take with them one of the Hollanders, who might speak with the *panico mudeliar*, but this was not thought advisable. This Matore Bellingham[95] and the whole district had, as the Hollanders afterwards learnt, within quite a short period, six or seven months before, been under the Portuguese, whom the inhabitants had resisted and risen against, so that the Portuguese had been obliged to retire to the Punto de Gallo and Colombo, which the Hollanders imagined to have occurred owing chiefly to the arrival of their ships[96].

The 10th July the yacht *Sphoera Mundi* with the boat of the *Holländische Hoff*[97] sailed for the river of Poligamme, and the next day after the admiral dispatched his boat to ascertain as early as possible from the yacht what sort of a situation there was round about that river, which returned the following day and reported that this river was about six miles distant from the harbour[98], where the yacht and the boat had thereupon anchored, so that no one could go out. They had also spoken with some [people] of the place, who had said that there was only one *champan* or ship in the river, for which a permit from the Hollanders had been requested. They also confirm [the statement] that three Dutch ships were lying at Jaffnapatan, which therefore was the more corroborated the longer the time that passed. Meanwhile however the Hollanders lay inactive before Matecalo, and accomplished nothing, except only that they

---

95. So printed: but there should be a comma after "Matore."

96. Cf. *C. Lit. Reg.* iv 165 note pp. Details of this rising against the Portuguese are lacking.

97. This is a mere variant of "*Hollandsche Zaum*," having the same meaning, (Dutch garden).

98. This last word (*Hafen* in the orig.) must be a mistranslation, or else Bree has made a slip. There was no "harbour" where the Dutch ships lay, only an open roadstead. As regards "the river of Poligamme," the distance given (say 24 miles) shows that by that name is meant the northern entrance to the backwater, the so-called "Batticaloa river." It appears to be called "the river of Poligamme," because by it Pálukámam was reached from the sea. The mouth of the "river is" actually from 28 to 30 miles distance from Karativu.

waited for their people from Candy, and as the latter did not so soon hurry back thither, they could not conceive or think what cause they had for their so long absence, especially as they had not received any letter or tidings either from them or from the Achinese envoy. Because then it did not seem advisable to depart from there before they had got back their people, or at least had received some tidings of them, they thought well, especially as the yacht with the one boat was lying before the river of Poligamme, to send of a boat to Jaffnapatan, in order that they might learn what kind of ships were to be found there. Soon the 13th following the boat of the vice-admiral was dispatched to ascertain this.

Furthermore as much time had elapsed, and they had now lain there inactive three months long, and had accomplished nothing useful, considering also that they had now been separated for seven months from their admiral and other ships, and had received no tidings of them, they resolved not to send any ships this time to the coast of Choromandel and the bay of Bengale[99] but as soon as they set out from there they would go to Achin, there to learn what tidings there were from Bantam and other places, and to act accordingly. The same day however there came an *arache* to the vice-admiral, and asked for two permits for two *champans* or ships that wished to come from Mattore or some of the adjacent places to the Hollanders with cinnamon, pepper and *arecca*, which they therefore let him have.

He said further however that the king of Matecalo would journey the following day to Tirecoy, a place situated some three or four miles south from there[100], where a great

99. B. V. has erroneously: "they therefore resolved to send a ship to the coast of Choromandel, and to proceed to Bengala."

100. Tirrukkóvil seems to have been visited by very few Europeans; and I know of no detailed description of the temple: in fact, the only one that I can find is that by Mr. Thomas Christie, who accompanied Governor North in his journey from Trincomalee to Matara in 1802, and whose notes are printed in Cordiner's *Ceylon* if. He say (p 137) :—"Tricoil is a considerable village, at which there is a Hindoo pagoda [sic] of very great antiquity. The pagoda is of considerable size, and built of brick and chunam, but is in bad repair: on the walls there is a great variety of sculpture coarsely executed. It is surrounded with two spacious courts, both of which we walked round, but were denied admittance into the pagoda On a swamy couch, which is kept in a shed without the courts, there are a great many obscene and unnatural scenes represented by rude carvings in wood."

festival was to be held[101], in honour of an idol or pagode there, which festival would last the whole of nine or ten days long, until the time of the full moon, where many thousands of persons would then assemble from all the surrounding places, both men and women and children: wherefore he wished to notify and inform the Hollanders that during that time no or very few fowls and fruits would come to the shore to be bartered. They hold this yearly throughout the whole island in various places.

The 15th following the boat returned from the yacht, which had sailed the previous day in the evening with the boat from Poligamme for Jaffnapatam.

The 20th however they saw on the shore a white flag of truce, at which they greatly rejoiced, hoping to receive letters and tidings from Candy, wherefore they forthwith sent thither two boats, which soon came back to the ships with an *arache* and a Dutchman, who brought letters from Jacob Corneliss, from which the Hollanders learnt that the aforesaid Jacob Corneliss had arrived at Candy the 29th of the past month together with the envoy, but he had not found the king there, who was in his camp at Sytabague, situated some 15 miles from Candy and 6 miles from Colombo [102]. After he had been informed of his arrival however he had commanded him to come to him; and when he came thither he was received right nobly by the king, who had greatly deplored the misfortune that had occurred at Matecalo through a misunderstanding and error, with the strongest promise henceforth to place a great and firm trust in the Dutch nation, and also as soon as possible to load two ships with cinnamon and pepper, as he had then already equipped some elephants with two *baeron* of cinnamon and two *baeren* of pepper to send to the Hollanders, half of which he wished to present to the Hollanders for kitchen use[103], and the other half as a sample. In addition he requested that another man should be dispatched to him, with whom he might effect

101. Cf. Rycks, s.d. 14 July.

102. "Sytubague" is, of course, Sítávaka: but for what purpose Vimaladharma had gone thither, I do not know.

103. Cf. de Weert's letter, supra, C1, towards the end.

the sale. All this, as the Hollanders could easily recognise and also very firmly believed, was idle hypocritical talk and promises, wherewith to detain them, in order with their presence to hold the Portuguese in check, and once more at sometime or other by treachery to make use of them: wherefore the Hollanders did not deem it advisable to remain there longer, and allow themselves to be led astray with idle and vain words or promises; so they were entirely of a mind, as soon as they should get back their man from Candy, whom they now expected daily, to set off again on their voyage, and go to Achin.

The 22nd there came to the vice-admiral one of those that had journeyed with Jacob Corneliss from Matecalo to Candy, who said that he had set out with him from Candy about eight days before, and had left him at Vintana, whence he had journeyed in advance to inform the Hollanders thereof: which however the Hollanders afterwards discovered to be untrue, since he had left Candy quite two days before Jacob Corneliss.

The 24th in the evening the aforesaid Jacob Corneliss came to the shore, and further to the vice-admiral, with a letter from the king, whom he had left in his camp at Sytabague, and had set out from Candy on the 15th instant. With him came the envoy, who had gone with him to the king, also some of the envoy's company, whom he had left all together at Matecalo, and would come on board ship the following day. There were also at Matecalo eight elephants laden with the abovementioned cinnamon and pepper. The letter of the king was nothing else than to detain them (the Hollanders) with a vain hope. There came back again however the same evening the yacht and the boat that had journeyed to Jaffnapatam, which brought tidings that they had found no ships.

The 25th following there came on board ship the *arache* and envoy from Candy together with some from Achin, who had much to say of the king of Candy and to belaud him, as that he would easily furnish two ships with lading, and would send the other two with his envoy to the mainland, where they also would be loaded. They further strongly

F 2

urged that the Hollanders would again dispatch some of the chief among them to Candy, there to speak with the king and effect the sale, who would forthwith give orders to collect the cinnamon and pepper from all parts. The Hollanders however would not allow themselves to be persuaded thereto, owing to the little trust they had, and that they should so often journey such a long way, by which then precious time would be lost. These envoys returned to land in the evening, and said they would come back to the shore the next day with some elephants and a *baer* of cinnamon as well as a *baer* of pepper, which the king had sent for the provision of the kitchen or for daily use ; the other two *baeren* of cinnamon and pepper were sent there as a sample, and were to remain at Matecalo until the sale of the rest were concluded so that they might then receive all together. At the same time they dispatched two boats, namely those of the vice-admiral and the ship called *Hollandia*, to the river of Poligamme, to see if they could there get by barter or buy some rice.

The 26th in the afternoon the aforesaid envoy together with the Achinese came on board ship once more, and brought with him the abovementioned cinnamon and pepper : they once again strongly urged that some of the Hollanders should be allowed to go to Candy with them, but they refused this and said that they had determined to depart at the earliest opportunity, and to betake themselves to a place where they hoped to be received and welcomed better and with more truth. Consequently the envoys must return the next day, when they would give them a letter for the king, and so dispatch them.

Those from Achin had before their journey to Candy often said that the deceased vice-admiral had promised their king at Achin that when they came to Zeylon he would advance them some money, to buy some precious stones and gems, up to some 20 *cathy*[104] of silver ; but as those in the council of war knew nothing thereof, they considered it to be inadvisable to do this, but since they had brought

104. That is, catties (Malay *kati*).

with them some sulphur from Achin[105], they promised to give them six *baeren* of this, to sell it to the king[106], and to use the money, until they came back to Achin, when the money was to be refunded. So they returned to land, and said they would come back to the shore the next day with some elephants to receive and load the sulphur.

The 27th in the afternoon they returned on board ship, to receive their dimissal and letters to the king, which were then given to them in the Dutch and Portuguese languages, of one substance or tenor. The Hollanders said in addition that they were to inform the king of Candy that, inasmuch as he desired henceforth to keep friendship with their people, and hoped to load two of their ships with cinnamon and pepper, he must collect all the cinnamon and pepper, so that, when any ships came thither into the harbour, he could forthwith deal with them, and he must do this with more truth and uprightness than had been shown to them, because means would not be wanting to them to take revenge on him. So they loaded the six *baeren* of sulphur, and in the evening returned to land. It is true that those from Achin were not altogether well pleased that they were not to return home again with them; but they were not yet dispatched, and it appeared that the king had in his hands some bales of cloth or silk to send over to the king of Achin, for which they must still wait. They gave them a letter for the king of Achin[107]. and so the Hollanders all together set sail at noon along the shore to the river of Poligamme, that they might come to the boat there: consequently in the evening, when they had sailed some six miles, they cast anchor before the abovesaid river of Poligamme.

The 29th early in the morning the boat of the ship *Hollandia* came out of the river to go to the ships, and brought some 600 *coquos*; it also reported that two of them had travelled up the river as far as Poligamme. which was about

105. Sulphur is not found in Achin, I believe.

106. For the manufacture of gunpowder, with which to carry on the war with the Portuguese.

107. And this is the last we hear of the Achin envoy and his suite. They probably returned home in a native vessel.

six miles, one of whom was a black or moor from the Portuguese ships, who had remained with them of his own free will, and could speak Portuguese and Malavarish well. These two, when they returned to the boat, had declared for a truth that the king of Poligamme had a tolerable quantity of pepper, which he wished to sell to them, for they themselves had seen a whole house full of pepper. Thereupon the Hollanders thought well to dispatch one of their under-merchants with the aforesaid black or moor to Poligamme to the king, to ascertain what pepper might be there, and these set out forthwith. Meanwhile the boat lay a quarter of a mile up the river before a village[108], where they daily bartered for rice, fowls, *cocos* and other fruits.

The 30th instant in the morning two small snips or boats came sailing to the ship *Hollandia*, which brought some fresh fish with them, and asked to view the interior of the ship, which was allowed them.

In the same manner there came on the 31st in the morning early many boats to the ship, with fish, rice, *coquos*, eggs, fowls, limes and other things to barter.

Soon after this moreover both the boats came out of the river again to the ship, in which also were the Hollanders, who had escaped in the night from Poligamme: these were well pleased that they had got away from there so easily, since they had not been so very welcome or acceptable, for indeed they brought nothing with them; and because they were apprehensive that it would have no good result for them, they made many promises to the king of giving him one thing and another on credit on account of some pepper that he promised to have ready in twenty days, at which time they would return thither, as he said that at that time no pepper was yet to be obtained there. So he had let the Hollanders go, and had given them a *modeliar*, who was to receive what they had promised him. This *modeliar* besides another *modeliar* from the village before which the boat had lain, together with seven other persons, came in a boat to the vice-admiral's ship, and the *modeliar* threw on to and

108. Perhaps Kalladi.

over the head of the vice-admiral a handful of gold cut small, and also put on his finger an inferior gold ring; they also brought with them a small basket of pepper and two pots full of honey as a sample or by way of bait, with the announcement of the very good affection and inclination of their king towards the Hollanders, hoping thus to obtain what had been promised the king by the Hollanders: but they soon saw well that they would get nothing there; so there was given to each one a small mirror, and they returned to land. The Hollanders also sent ashore with them the abovementioned moor, who had said that he had seen at Poligamme a whole house full of pepper, because he had uttered such a lie to them: and so in the evening about an hour before sunset they set sail with a westerly wind, directing their course east-south-east for Achin.

DESCRIPTION OF CEYLON[109].

The island of Zeylon is fairly fertile in rice and all kinds of fruits, such as *bonanes*, *batatas*, *ananassen*, limes, oranges, &c., on the coast it is true there is not much, but further inland there is a great abundance and quantity of *coquos*, fowls, eggs, deer, wild boars, oxen and buffaloes, &c. However as regards the oxen and buffaloes, one dare not kill or slaughter them at all there, nay they also would not sell these to the Hollanders, as they hold such for a great sin; they use them only for work, and when any of them die of themselves, they are accustomed to bury them[110]. The best cinnamon grows in this island, especially around Colombo; there is also pepper, which is very good; much wax is also found there, and various precious stones, in particular rubies. The inhabitants there are heathens and idolaters: they have everywhere in the country many idols,

109. B. V. omits what follows, and says:—"Here it would not be out of place to describe the island of Zeylon, but as this has been done in the foregoing voyage under the command of Joris van Spilbergen, we will therefore refer the reader thereto, and proceed with our begun description."

110. Cf. Rÿcks.

which they call *pagodes*[111]—these are images sometimes of men, but sometimes of other animals, with which they make very much ado, and hold many great festivals to honour these, and that indeed at various times of the year, with dancing, singing, leaping, and much playing of shawms and other instruments.

[112]The Hollanders saw in the town of Candy idols of five or six fathoms high, well proportioned and ingeniously made, which they held to be made after the measurement of Adam, since the length and breadth of the feet agree wholly and entirely with the footstep of Adam that the king had caused to be brought into the town from a mountain that was situated not far from there : they are seven and a half spans long, and three and half broad[113]. They said it was the footsteps of the first man.

All these idols or images have each their fixed attributes and power the one over the fruits of the land, the other over the rain, others over the wind and tempest at sea, and so forth ; and they say that they are set or placed by God over these, and have obtained such power ; they acknowledge and do not deny that there is one God, who has made and created everything ; they burn their dead before and in the presence of their *bramenes* or priests, with many ceremonies, in their best clothes, of which they have very few, since they go about naked, except for a cotton cloth wrapped round the private parts[114]. As to the people that dwell near the sea, they seem to be Malavars, and also use the same language, and for the most part long hanging ears with big holes, in

111. This is, of course, a gross error, the word *pagode* being unknown is Ceylon until the Portuguese introduced it, and certainly neither the Sinhalese nor the Tamils described either their images or their temples by such a word. (Cf. de Weert's letter supra, C1, note 49).

112. The statements in this paragraph are taken over from de Weert's letter.

113. Both the first and the second editions have " long." Sá e Menezes (*Reb. de Cey.* 16), describing Adam's Peak, speaks of a slab in which is a human foot-print " somewhat larger that the ordinary ones, as states Diego de Conto from sure information : though others make it three spans in length, and the Calvinists, with their wonted deceit, make it seven." The reference is evidently to this passage.

114. Cf. Rycks infra.

which are some rings of lead, copper, or gold, according to opportunity. The children have for the most part large heavy leaden rings hanging in their ears, that they may in time acquire long ears, which with them is a great beauty and peculiar ornament[115]. These people have their kings at Panane, Matecalo, and Poligamme, all of whom are subject to the king of Candy, who is a great and sworn enemy of the Portuguese.

[116]How the present king came to the throne, of this the Hollanders received the following account. Fifteen miles from Candy, and six miles from Colombo, lies a town named Sitabague, the king of which about thirty years before became very powerful and warred with those of Colombo, and also with the king of Candy. When he had conquered the town of Candy, and got possession of the whole country, the king of Candy, with a little daughter who was still a child, and this present king, who was then quite young and was the son of a *modeliar*, fled to Manar, and placed himself under the protection of the Portuguese. From there the boy was sent to Goa and made a Christian, being called by the name of Don Juan de Austria. Afterwards he came to the fortress of Colombo, and was there made a captain over some blacks or moors : so he remained and dwelt there several years longer, until the time when those of Candy and the whole country around there began to rebel against the king of Sitabague. The Portuguese were mindful of that opportunity, and because the king of Candy had died, they sent a body of men to the help of those of Candy, and among others also this Don Juan, although at the beginning they did not wish to let him go. This Don Juan when he came into the country obtained a great following, whereby he began to consider how he might become entirely the ruler of the country : he gave little heed to the Portuguese, and

115. According to Knox (*Hist Rel.* 89-90) the fashion of long-lobed ears went out in the reign of Raja Sinha II, who did not favour it.

116. What follows does not appear in the edition of 1605. It is founded partly on the historical summary given by the Spilbergen diarist and partly on verbal or written information derived from other sources.

finally turned his force against the king of Sitabague, whom he then also conquered. Some years after this the Portuguese came into the country with many men, and brought with them into the country the daughter of the deceased king, who had also been made a Christian by them, who was a lawful heir thereto, in order that by this means she might get possession of the country: they immediately took possession of the town of Candy, whereupon this Don Juan fled to the mountains, where be again collected his force, fell upon the Portuguese and defeated them, so that few of them escaped. After this he took the king's daughter in marriage as queen, and although against her wish prosecuted the war[117]. He got by her two children, a son and a daughter, who is at present five or six years old, and are lawful heirs to the kingdom.

After the Hollanders then had sailed again from the shore or river of Poligamme, and had directed their course east-south-east, with a south-west wind, about the 9th of August they sighted land, and in the evening came into the harbour before Achin, where they then found their two ships the *Stern* and *Vlissengen*[118].......

The 11th August two of the Hollanders went to the town, there to deliver the letter to the king that they had brought from Zeylon through the secretary Pongolo Corquon [119], with whom they rode to the king's palace, sitting behind him on an elephant with some gifts that they wished to present to the king. When they came to the gate of the palace the Pongolo Corquon went beforehand to the king, but they remained standing there, and awaited his *chappe*[120], after which they also went in, and found the king sitting

117. Either the editor or the printer has made a muddle here of the fact that Dom Joáo married Dona Catharina against her will, (her repugnance being founded on very good reason). It is not likely that she expressed any opinion as regards the prosecution of the war, and certainly Dom Joáo would have paid little heed thereto had she done so.

118. See supra, note 88.

119. Pongolo is the Malay *pengulu*, headman, chief. Davies mentions this secretary as "Corcoun" (Purchas, 1905, ed. ii, 314)

120. Licence or passport (see *Hob.-Job.* s.v. "Chop").

and looking out up above, according to his custom[121]. They made him reverence after the manner of the country, presented the gifts to him, and seated themselves under a shed opposite to him, putting their legs crosswise over one another like tailors[122]. The secretary moreover sat in his place, who translated into the Malavarish[123] language and then delivered to the king the letter brought by the Hollanders written from Zeylon, from which he learnt the situation and the position of his envoys. As regards the misfortune that had befallen them in Zeylon however and the death of the vice-admiral, he had already had full information, namely when the ships the *Stern* and *Vlissengen* had arrived; he then showed himself much grieved on account of it, and deplored it very vehemently.

ANNEXURE D3.

D3.—DIARY OF JAN JACOB RŸCKS.

Jan Jacob R¨cks, from whose journal[1] (preserved in the Hague archives) the following excerpts are made, held some position on board the ship *Hollandia*, through what it was, does not appear[2]. De Jonge, who utilised this diary[3] in his *Opkomst van het Ned Gezuj* iii 10-16, calls him " one of the skippers," but with what authority I do not know. His journal is not to be compared in fulness of detail with that of Bree (judging by the portion relating to Ceylon); but nevertheless is of value in supplementing the narrative

121. The king of Achin was accustomed to sit in a balcony of his palace when giving audience.

122. Cf. Davis, in Purchas ii 320.

123. This should, of course, be " Malayish."

1. It extends from 17 June, 1602 to 26 August, 1603. Mr. van Riemsdÿk, the general archivist at the Hague, informs me that at the beginning of the journal is the following note :—" Ick Jan Jacp Rÿcx van Opmeer hoert toe dit boack. Die het vint eer verloern is, die sterve eer hij sieck is " (" To I (Sic) Jan Jaep Rÿcx of Opmeer belongs this book. Who finds it ere it is lost, may he die ere he is sick."

2. Judging by his entries for 27 June to 13 July we might infer that he had charge of the commissariat!

3. The quotations that de Jonge gives are for the most part paraphrases in his own words.

of the latter, especially as regards the massacre of de Weert and his companions. He appears to have been not very well educated, his Dutch being often uncouth and ungrammatical.

The 25th [April, 1603] we arrived in the roadstead at Matecaloe[1], and it is a dangerous shore, so that one can with difficulty see where the roadstead is, because Matekelo lies a short mile[2] inland. But there is a mountain inland, that we call *Hang lip*[3]. When this is between west and west-by-north of you, then you are in the roadstead, and one lies there in 7 and 8 or 9 fathoms water[4], excellent bottom—fine sand. Matekeloe lies in 7½ degrees, and in a little less than thirteen degrees of longitude[5].

The 26th our vice-admiral went ashore with 100 men with a banner flying and with a drum and trumpets, and so went to the king of Maetekeloo, and thus arrived before that king's palace, and there they were honorably welcomed and very honorably received; and our people there saw much novelty, both in their eating and in their idols, because all that was brought to our people to eat was laid upon a large leaf of a *benantes*[6]*-tree*, such as rice, or fish, or fowls, honey, all together in a heap. And the inhabitants of the country looked at us with wonder, both as regards our clothes and our arms, our banners, drums, trumpets. So that we left there in peace and friendship, so that on the 27th we came on board again with all our people, safe and sound.

The inhabitants of the country, when a man dies there, he is forthwith burnt, and his wife burnt with him, because

---

1. It will be noticed that Rijcks spells this name in a variety of ways. The Dutch very soon abandoned the spelling with the correct initial letter *M*, and adopted the erroneous form with *B*, which the Portuguese invariably used.

2. Lit. "a milekin." Cf. Bree's statement as to the distance.

3. Meaning "blubber-lip." This ugly name did not persist, the Dutch taking over the Portuguese name, *Capello de Frade*, and translating it as *Nunnikskap*. The mountain still bears the name of Friars Hood (see G3).

4. From Karativu looking inland Friar's Hood lies west by north. What the depth of the sea off Karativu is I do not know.

5. Sammanturei lies in about 81° 50' E., 7° 20' N.

6. Rijcks in every case spells banana in this odd fashion, with an intrusive *t*.

otherwise she is considered unhappy; when a woman dies there, she is immediately burnt, but not her husband. Those are the customs of the island of Seloon[7].

The 29th three of our sloops left, namely our vice-admiral's sloop and the Enchuyser man[8] his sloop: they sailed for Pannevee[9], in order to inquire there concerning some things, because Panevee lies 7 miles[10] more southerly than the roadstead of Maetekeloe does, because in Pannevee is also a king, and he is the father of the king of Battekeloo[11]. But the sloop of the *Vlissengen* sailed for Poelegame[12], and there is also a king, and he bears himself very valiantly[13].

In the island of Seyloon is everywhere provision enough of fowls, of *cockes*[14], of *benantes*, eggs, fish, harts, hinds, pigs. A hen or cock one buys cheap for the value of a half-stiver, as also for a little lead, for mirrors, scissors, old linen, handkerchiefs, old felt caps. So that one could get by barter for little value provision enough, but it was forbidden to us that we should in the least degree barter or trade, the which was done in order that we should cause no rise in price there. Then were three men placed on land there in the warehouse[15], in order to trade in everything to the profit of the ships and for victualing.

In the island of Seylloen are all kinds of birds, such as peacocks, storks, starlings, sparrows, larks, snipe, peewits, in fact every kind of bird that one could think of; all kinds of beasts, foxes, apes, rabbits, harts, hinds, in fact all that one can think of[16] buffaloes, elephants. Yea, it is the best

---

7. Rÿcks appears to have imagined that all the inhabitants of Ceylon were Hindus, like the Tamils he met with at this place.

8. The "Enchuyser man" was Jacob Pietersz, commander of the *Hollantse Tuyn* and successor to de Weert as vice-admiral (see below under 4 June).

9. Panawr (see Bree's journal supra, note 38).

10. Bree says ten miles.

11. Bree does not mention this relationship.

12. Pālukāmam (see Bree's journal, note 37).

13. Cf. what Rÿcks says below of this man's behaviour during the massacre.

14. Coconuts (cf. under 27 June).

15. In orig. *Loesy*, from Portuguese *lo ja*, shop. Under the form *logie* it was adopted by the Dutch in the 17th century to denominate what the English called a "factory" (from the Portuguese *feitoria*)

16. Some of the birds and beasts named are not found in Ceylon.

cinnamon country that there is in the whole world, or where more cinnamon grows; but through war and fighting that the king of Kange[17] has there against the Portuguese, the land is uncultivated, because the Portuguese have the best portion of the island, because they have the castle of Collombe which is so strong, that the walls are almost a rod thick, so that it is hard to capture; and they have Ponte Gaele, which is also a fine fortress[18]. For [in] the island of Seloon are seven kings, of whom the king of Kange is the chief, because he is like emperor, because Kange that is the chief town of Seyloon, because the king of Cange is Christian[19], but the other six kings[20] are not. The king of Kange received his Christianity in Goa, because he dwelt there four years[21] with the Portuguese when he was young, and because it [*sic*] was the son of the old king of Kandy[22], and the Portuguese had peace there, because they caused to be done all that they wished, because they departed from the territory of the old king. So then the son came from Goa, and was well educated, spoke good Latin and good Portuguese, and after the death of his father he was king of Kange, and again withstood the Portuguese, because otherwise they would have driven him out of his territory so that they do one another much injury.

MAY

The 2nd came our sloop from Poellegame, and the king of Poelegaeme asked heartily to see our vice-admiral, the which took place.

17. This is another of the writer's odd spellings: how he came to substitute a *g* for the *a* it is difficult to imagine.

18. Rijcks got these exaggerated ideas of the strength of the forts of Colombo and Galle from native reports. Contrast what the Spanish captain Antonio Martins told his king (*M. L. R.* iv, 125-26).

19. He had long ere this adjured his profession of Christianity, and had returned to Buddhism.

20. Of these six, three were doubtless the "kings" of Matecalo. Pálukámam and Pánawa mentioned below, and other two were perhaps the princes of Matale and Uva, while the sixth may have been the king of Jaffna, though this is doubtful.

21. 1588-92.

22. The Spilbergen diarist was better informed as to the parentage of Dom João (see *C. L. R.* vi 333).

The 4th our vice-admiral went to Poelegamme, and was there well received, because the king of Poelegame had never in his life seen any Dutch[23].

The 5th the vice-admiral came on board again, safe and sound, with all those that had sailed with him.

The 6th it was resolved by the broad council that we should go on shore and shoot buffaloes, oxen and cows, to which the inhabitants would not consent, because there they kill no buffaloes, nor any cows, nor oxen, because they live as long as they may, and then when they die, they bury them, because they consider them as holy as their gods. And the dung that comes from the buffaloes, that they burn, and with the ashes they smear their foreheads. and our people shot quite 7 or 8 buffaloes. But the inhabitants said against us, that as many buffaloes as we shot, so many souls were damned, because they imagine that the buffaloes have souls, because they say that when buffaloes die of themselves, then the souls are not damned, but when we shoot them dead then they are damned. So that every day they complained to the king of Batekeloe of the violence that we used towards them, so that we became bad friends with the king and the inhabitants, the which we did not much trouble about[24], because we had the king of Cange in our favour, because all the kings of Seylon fear the king of Cange more than a schoolboy his master, because the king of Kandie is a severe king and executes stern justice[25], so that they all fear him.

The 14th there came there two Dutchmen from the king of Cande with his chief general[26], who came for help to our vice-admiral, in order to besiege Ponte Gaele and Collombe by sea, in order that the Portuguese should afford them no relief, because the king of Kandia had over a hun-

23. He is not mentioned by the Spilbergen diarist. According to Bree, his reception of de Weert did not come up to expectation.

24. From Bree's statements one would judge that the Dutch did trouble over the matter.

25. The writer little thought when he penned this that the king's "stern justice" would be executed on the Dutch themselves.

26. Apparently Manoe Dias (see supra, de Weert's letter, note 52).

dred thousand men in the field, whom he would bring by land before Ponte Gaele and Collombe. Because the king of Kandia would pay for it quite ten-fold in cinnamon and pepper because the king of Candia has enough cinnamon in his territory, but the Portuguese invade him fiercely.

The 16th in the morning we saw a Portuguese ship, which came from Cotsyn, she was quite 300 lasts in burden, and had nothing in her but ballast, and intended tc sail to Neegepotan in order to lade rice there, the which with our company we captured and plundered her, and they told us that three more ships were coming up that way, and were also from Cotseyn and were not above 5 or 6 miles from us.

The 17th we again saw a Portuguese ship, and it was one of the three ships, and we weighed our anchor with our five ships, namely the *Hollandia*, the *Sterre*, the *Hollanse Twyn*, the ship *Vlyssingen*, *den Haes*[27], and in the evening we were close to her, and at night she escaped us; and in the morning we met another, and hat we captured and brought her into the roadstead to our vice-admiral, and she was also plundered. Then we had there now two.

The 19th in the morning we again saw another ship south of us, and she was likewise of the company: we sailed towards her with our two or three and brought her also into the roadstead beside the others. The same evening the *Hollantse Tuyn* shot our ship[28] through her main-mast, and the slivers broke out, so that the third part of the mast was in pieces. And the same evening the *Hollantse Tuyn* put to sea with two shallops, in order to seek for that ship that had escaped us by night, because she must again approach the land, because she likewise intended for Neegepotan, because she was likewise a ship of 300 lasts.

The 23rd the *Hollantse Tuyn* came again into the roadstead with the two shallops, and had captured the carrack altogether, but the Portuguese had gone off from her in

27. A curious error, and worse even than that of Artus in Bree's diary, since the name of the ship *Der Goes* is here transformed into *The Hare*.

28. The *Hollandia*. Bree does not mention this accident.

their shallop and had taken with them all the money, and their valuable jewels and their goods, and they left therein some 60 old slaves. So she came into the roadstead besides us. Then we had all four of them. Two were each of 300 lasts and the other two were of about 70 lasts, and one was a new ship, and intended for Syna[29], and had in her much merchandise, the which was all prize

So these four ships were plundered, and two of them were allowed to go with all the people, and the other two were allowed to drive on shore and there be knocked to pieces, but from one we took the main-mast and with the one half made checks for our main-mast, and with the [other] half made checks likewise for our bowsprit, because it was a main-mast of one of the big ships. Then from the other of the little ships the *Sterre* took the main-mast, and made therefrom a bowsprit. Thus two of the Portuguese ships perished and the other two with all the people sailed for Negepotan on the 29th.

JUNE.

The first day the vice-admiral went ashore with two hundred armed men, with two ensigns, [and] with two drums and twelve trumpets, and handsomely dressed, to receive with honour the great king of Cange : thus we marched to Matèkeloe with a great display. When we were come to Matekeloe, the king of Cange had not yet arrived, so we proceeded a little out of Maetekeloe. There the king of Candia came towards us, and our vice-admiral fell at his feet and did him reverence, and the king of Kandia also received our vice-admiral friendlily. Then the king set his men in a ring, and we with our men marched around thrice three by three in one file within the king's troops, and shot terrifically, so that there was a great ovation, because there were then three met together, namely, the king of Candia, the king of Pamnesee[30], [and] the king of Bate-

---

29. China. Bree does not tell us this.
30. Pånawa.

keloe, and the which had such a bad issue for us, because it cost us fully 47 men[31]. Then we marched forward thus to Battekeloe, and conducted him to the king of Battekeloe's palace, and we knew of no danger, but we went into an enclosed garden where stood a number of huts and houses, and there we ate a little fish and a little rice that the king of Battekeloe presented us with. When now we went to eat something, then we shot once again all round, or then we went to sit and eat a little.

When we had now eaten a little, and the vice-admiral was with the king, then he came to us and desired of the rest of us that we should go on board ship and come again in the morning, and we should convoy the king on the shore near to the ships ; and he kept with him 25 or 26 men, because he recked of no danger. Among the 25 men were eight trumpeters, two upper merchants and two or three assistants and lads. So now we went on board and left the vice-admiral with the aforesaid men at Batekeloe, and we imagined nothing else than that they would speak with each other how they were to arrange that, and how much cinnamon and pepper the king would have to deliver to us.

Because our vice-admiral himself had been in Candie about four months before, and had then promised the king of Candie that he would help him by water, and whatever Portuguese the vice-admiral captured at sea........[32] Atsÿn and Celon ; because the vice-admiral was there with only his three ships, and then he came to Atsÿn. There came the vice-admiral then to us, and then we lay there[33] with our three Hollandt ships and two privateer ships[34] of Moesteroen's[35] from Seelandt. Then the vice-admiral with his council bought one of the freebooter ships, and then we went with our seven ships [and] three shallops to the island of Celon in order to help the king of Selon with our ships against Ponte Gaele and against Colomb.... and that with

31. See further on.
32. Lacuna in ms.
33. At Achin.
34. The *Schaep* and the *Ram*.
35. Moucheron's.

an agreement that we should have peace with the king of Candia and should come every year with two or three ships to receive the cinnamon there and the peppe· and that with great promises and the most honorable intentions.

Now on 25 April we came to Ceylon before Batekeloe into the roadstead, and in Matekeloe received the king of Candia with honour, the which turned out ill for us. Now then I shall tell of the admiral, and how it befell him in Ma teloe.

When then we returned from the vice-admiral and left him with the king of Candia with 25 or 26 men, as was before related, then the vice-admiral spoke with the king at every opportunity, because the vice-admiral was not afraid to give his opinion against the king. So they drank round all together with one another with one accord, and the vice-admiral became intoxicated[36], so that they fell to abusing each other ; and it annoyed the king of Candia so much because our vice-admiral had let the Portuguese go, so that he took it in bad part, because the vice-admiral had promised him to keep [them], and did not do so, and his people, who incited him, so that he consented, and they murdered the vice-admiral with all those that were with him, and pursued us as far as the shore, and killed all that they caught ; and the king of Poelegamme lay near us in the woods with other 300 men armed, and he also received word that he was to kill all the Dutch that he could come by[37] : so that we lost 47 persons and six mortally wounded, but they recovered again altogether[38]. This now having been done, there was complete enmity, and we not knowing for certain that such came to us thence, because we imagined that all was friendly, and it changed to enmity. And this happened on 1 June, 1603.

---

36. Cf. the statement of Baldaeus, infra, F5, at note 8.

37. Rijcks is the only authority that mentions the participation of the "king" of Pálukámam in the massacre

38. A rather Irish statement! The Spilbergen diarist has it that all 53 were killed.

JUNE.

The 2nd in e evening there c there a le the king of Cand [saying] for what r n he had do and that it carr out owing to [the f that he [the admiral] had le the Portuguese go, w were his mo enemies ; because had we not let the Portuguese go, it wou not have happene to us ; but the king of Candia imagin that he was betrıed, since the vice-admiral had promise him much and ha fulfilled little thereof ; because the king of Cande had meat to keep the Portuguese, and thought thereby to release his son, because the Portuguese had captured him[39], so that the king of Candia let himself be incited by the rest of his [people] so that a wholesale massacre took place there, which the .king of Candia greatly regrets, and desires on account of sorrow still to give cinnamon and pepper and the rest that he had promised. Now the same day he wrote again to the rest of us a letter harsh and severe. They wrote to each other during full sixteen days[40].

[[41]The 4th day of the same month Jacop Pietersz of Enchuÿsen, who was commander, of the ships the *Hollantsche Tuÿn*, was chosen by the broad council as vice-admiral].

The 17th[42] day there came there an ambassador with a Dutchman as well on behalf of the king of Candia, to make peace, and he would promise us a large number of quintals of cinnamon and several bales of pepper, which he would put on board our ships ere we should do him any services.

The 19th a man[43] was appointed by the rest of us [to go] there, and took with him the Dutchman that came from the king.

The 20th in the evening there put to sea three of our ships, namely, the *Sterre* and *Vlyssingen* sailed for Atsÿn, and *den Raes*[44] for Bantum.

---

39. See infra, F1, note 7.
40. For details see Bree's journal *supra*.
41. In the original this paragraph comes after the entry for 19 June. I have transferred it to this place for convenience.
42. Bree says it was on the 16th.
43. Jacob Cornelisz, according to Bree.
44. Read "*der Goes.*"

No. 81.—day w... day. The ...
...ut, eac... or 150 fowls, wi... quite ...
ships bargain... pine-apples[45], rice-cakes[46],—or
Holl... benan...
nut...
e...

JULY.

The 1st bargained for some 80 fowls and other goods of a like kind.

The 4th day bargained for some 130 fowls and other provision of a similar character.

The 7th day bargained for some 160 fowls with other provision besides.

The 10th day bargained for 210 fowls with other provision besides.

The 13th day bargained for 104 with enough of other provision besides.

The 14th day there was on the island a great festival that never comes at one time in the year. They then go with everybody to Tiercowil in order there to pray to their *peegoeden*[47]. But Tiercowil lies 9 miles from Batekelo, and the festival lasts 12 days, for during the 12 days we could obtain no provision, because they had all gone to their *pagodt*, in order to hold the festival[48].

(*To be continued*)

---

45. In orig. "*pinges*" the meaning of which I am doubtful about.

46. Or, "rice, cakes."

47. See Bree, s.d. 13 July.

48. Here the Ceylon portion of this diary ends, except that Rÿcks records that on 28 July, ere they set sail from the roadstead of "Maetekeloe," the Dutch bought some more fowls as provisions. It will be noticed that he records only the *Hollandia's* purchases! so, that, if the other two ships' supplies of fowls were on the same scale, the crews of the three vessels must have had a surfeit of chicken by the time they reached Achin

that it was Colombo, the chief place and fort that the Portuguese had in Ceylon. And he asked him further regarding every circumstance and as to how many men lay therein; he answered that there were about 400 Portuguese soldiers there, and that there dwelt there several thousand Indian Christians[3], who held with the Portuguese.

And when the council had assembled it was voted by the majority that they might gain honour enough there, if they tried with the fleet to conquer such a place and fort as Colombo. As almost the whole council understood the matter thus, that they were fully authorized by their interpretation of the secret instructions to take that work in hand; as in the secret instructions is stated that they must not remain lying in Ceylon more than five or six days, unless they saw that there were some considerable profits to be made there[4] that was understood by the council as considerable profits, and that it was sufficiently said that they might attack the tow... and fortress of Colombo[5]. The which the admiral ... stood wholly otherwise, and therefore would in no... consent thereto, because it seemed to him that ... able profits were much more likely to tur... loss, because, as is said above, that if o... a place, of which no one of all those ... any knowledge, that one would t... so greatly imperil and place ... conquest of the Archip... would have to be a... knowledge? ... their noble ...

JUNE.

The 2nd in the evening there came there a letter from the king of Candia [saying] for what reason he had done that, and that it came about owing to [the fact] that he [the vice-admiral] had let the Portuguese go, who were his mortal enemies; because, had we not let the Portuguese go, it would not have happened to us; but the king of Candia imagined that he was betrayed, since the vice-admiral had promised him much and had fulfilled little thereof; because the king of Cande had meant to keep the Portuguese, and thought thereby to release his son, because the Portuguese had captured him[39], so that the king of Candia let himself be incited by the rest of his [people] so that a wholesale massacre took place there, which the king of Candia greatly regrets, and desires on account of sorrow still to give cinnamon and pepper and the rest that he had promised. Now the same day he wrote again to the rest of us a letter harsh and severe. They wrote to each other during full sixteen days[40].

[[41]The 4th day of the same month Jacop Pietersz of Enchuÿsen, who was commander of the ships the *Hollantsche Tuÿn*, was chosen by the broad council as vice-admiral].

The 17th[42] day there came there an ambassador with a Dutchman as well on behalf of the king of Candia, to make peace, and he would promise us a large number of quintals of cinnamon and several bales of pepper, which he would put on board our ships ere we should do him any services.

The 19th a man[43] was appointed by the rest of us [to go] there, and took with him the Dutchman that came from the king.

The 20th in the evening there put to sea three of our ships, namely, the *Sterre* and *Vlyssingen* sailed for Atsÿn, and *den Raes*[44] for Bantum.

---

39. See infra, F1, note 7.
40. For details see Bree's journal *supra*.
41. In the original this paragraph comes after the entry for 19 June. I have transferred it to this place for convenience.
42. Bree says it was on the 16th.
43. Jacob Cornelisz, according to Bree.
44. Read "*der Goes.*"

The 27th day we began again to trade with our three ships turn about, each its day. The first day for our ship *Hollandia* we bargained for 150 fowls, with quite 800 *kockus* nuts and *benantus*, pineapples[45], rice-cakes[46],—of everything.

JULY.

The 1st bargained for some 80 fowls and other goods of a like kind.

The 4th day bargained for some 130 fowls and other provision of a similar character.

The 7th day bargained for some 160 fowls with other provision besides.

The 10th day bargained for 210 fowls with other provision besides.

The 13th day bargained for 104 with enough of other provision besides.

The 14th day there was on the island a great festival that never comes at one time in the year. They then go with everybody to Tiercowil in order there to pray to their *peegoeden*[47]. But Tiercowil lies 9 miles from Batekelo, and the festival lasts 12 days, for during the 12 days we could obtain no provision, because they had all gone to their *pagodt*, in order to hold the festival[48].

(*To be continued*)

---

45. In orig. "*pinges*" the meaning of which I am doubtful about.

46. Or, "rice, cakes."

47. See Bree, s.d. 13 July.

48. Here the Ceylon portion of this diary ends, except that Rÿcks records that on 28 July, ere they set sail from the roadstead of "Maetekeloe," the Dutch bought some more fowls as provisions It will be noticed that he records only the *Hollandia's* purchases! so, that, if the other two ships' supplies of fowls were on the same scale, the crews of the three vessels must have had a surfeit of chicken by the time they reached Achin

THE EARLIEST DUTCH VISITS TO CEYLON[1]

BY DONALD FERGUSON.

Continued from Vol. XXXI., No. 81., p. 179.

21st November, 1604.—Having sighted the land of Ceylon the admiral assembled his council of war, to resolve if they should sail on forward with the fleet or if they should approach the land, because they were in great anxiety that they would not very well be able to reach the strait of Malaca, since it began to veer to the east *moussoen* and the wind began at times to blow from the east; but it was resolved that they should go and anchor before an inhabited town that they saw lying in front, where they rode. And while riding in 10 fathoms, the admiral caused the old Portuguese prisoner, who was captured before Calicuth with the galliot[2], to be brought from the ship *Amsterdam*, and asked him what kind of a town or city it was that he lay before. The Portuguese answered

1 The extract here given is translated from No. VII. of the "Documenten voor de geschiedenis der Nederlanders in het Oosten," mentioned above. It consists of the journal, so far as it exists, of Steven van der Hagen, the admiral of the fleet of 12 ships that left Holland for the East on 18th December, 1603. The whole of the journal preceding the passages here quoted is missing,—a grievous loss, not compensated for by the survival of the diary of Hendrik Jansz. Craen, a large part of which is printed by de Jonge in his *Opkomst* ii. 164-204. See extracts from this infra, notes 11, 12).

According to his instructions (printed as No. IV of the "Documenten,") van der Hagen proceeded from the coast of Africa to Goa and passed down the west coast of India, doing all the damage he could to Portuguese shipping, and seeking the friendship and alliance of various native rulers He was also ordered, "the *mousson* being past," to "go along the coast of Malabar to the island of Ceylon," and then: "Having come under the island of Ceylon, they shall remain there only 5 or 6 days, unless there were the appearance of making some considerable profits." Accordingly on 21st November, 1604 the fleet of ten ships (two had left the fleet at the Cape of Good Hope for Mauritius, and two had been sent to Gujarat for purposes of trade") appeared in sight of Columbo,—the first Dutch vessels that had ever been in that offing. I can find no reference by any Portuguese writer to this visit.)

2 On 30th October (see Craen's diary, in *Opkomst* ii. 168, where the captured Portuguese vessel is called a frigate).

that it was Colombo, the chief place and fort that the Portuguese had in Ceylon. And he asked him further regarding every circumstance and as to how many men lay therein; he answered that there were about 400 Portuguese soldiers there, and that there dwelt there several thousand Indian Christians[3], who held with the Portuguese.

And when the council had assembled it was voted by the majority that they might gain honour enough there, if they tried with the fleet to conquer such a place and fort as Colombo. As almost the whole council understood the matter thus, that they were fully authorized by their interpretation of the secret instructions to take that work in hand; as in the secret instructions is stated that they must not remain lying in Ceylon more than five or six days, unless they saw that there were some considerable profits to be made there[4] that was understood by the council as considerable profits, and that it was sufficiently said that they might attack the town and fortress of Colombo[5]. The which the admiral understood wholly otherwise, and therefore would in no manner consent thereto, because it seemed to him that such considerable profits were much more likely to turn to considerable loss, because, as is said above, that if one should attack such a place, of which no one of all those that were in the fleet had any knowledge, that one would there so plainly without reason so greatly imperil and place in hazard the fleet, whereby the conquest of the Archipelago of Ambona and other places[6], would have to be abandoned, of which the admiral had the knowledge[7], and of what great importance this was to their noble and mighty highnesses the States General, His

3 See further on, where the same number is given for the Portuguese soldiers, the native Christian militia being reckoned at 6,000. In 1615, according to a letter of Gijsbrecht van Zuylen's from Medamahanuwara, there were only about 150 Portuguese soldiers in Columbo.

4 See the quotation from the instructions in note 1 above.

5 A most extraordinary and far-fetched interpretation of the instruction, which van der Hagen did quite right to resist.

6 One of the principal duties with which van der Hagen was charged.

7 He had been at the Moluccas in 1600, in command of a fleet of three ships (see *Opkomst* ii. 226-9).

Excellency and the East India Company. Whereupon many words passed between the admiral and the council of war, who said to them that he was admiral, who would have to answer for all going amiss on land. Wherefore he would not consent to that, nor also could he find from the instructions that they were authorized to do so; and since he found that almost all of the council were disposed to take in hand such wrong work, the admiral requested of the council a writing signed by them all, wherein was stated that they absolved him of all blame that might be laid upon him on account of that, it resulting therewith that he be able to defend and answer for himself before their noble and mighty highnesses the States-General, His Excellency and the East India Company; and he having this from them, then would he willingly be the first to make the expedition to land, because he said he did not hold his body and life dearer than another his. Thereupon they altogether remained silent without anyone's answering thereto. And this was now the third time that the admiral was so treated by his council of war, who had sought to persuade and embarrass him with unnecessary, unprofitable and unauthorized conquests,—the first time before Mossambique, the second time before Cananor[8], and the third time before Colombo. But it was quite another thing that moved them to this: it was those that sailed on the ships that were destined to sail for Patane and Bantam[9], these had a great dislike of the Ambonese and Moluckese voyage, therefore they stuck to each other, in order to persuade the admiral to the aforesaid affairs, in order to be released from the Ambonese and Moluckese voyage. And being thus occupied with this matter, there come one of the boats alongside bringing a captured Indian, of San Thome by birth, whom they had taken out of a *pangay*[10], that they had chased to shore, from which the Portuguese had sprung

8 Owing to the loss of the first portion of van der Hagen's journal details of the first two disagreements are wanting to us.

9 By the instructions, three ships were to go to Patani, and one to Bantam.

10 A small sailing canoe (see *Hobson-Jobson* s. vv. 'Pangara, Pangaia').

over board, swimming to land[11]. The admiral examined and questioned the Indian regarding every circumstance, who also said that in Colombo lay four hundred Portuguese and that there dwelt there about 6,000 Christian Indians, the which agreed with the statement of the old Portuguese prisoner. And all being further considered between the admiral and his council, it was resolved that they should at the first opportunity proceed with the fleet to Achyn, Malaca and Johor, and from there to Ambona and Moluken, in order there to take in hand better and more profitable things than certainly would have been got from Colombo[12]

31st December.—Then came the admiral a little before mid-day with the fleet into the road at Bantam, where he found the yacht *Medenblick*[13], which had lain there only eight days, and the admiral learnt there how all things stood throughout the whole of India, as also besides of the ill faring of Sibolt de Weert with his men, who in Ceylon were all smitten dead, whereby the admiral now understood why the Samorijn,

---

11 Craen's diary has :—" 21st November. The wind northerly and saw in the morning the island of Selon, towards which we set our course, east and east by north, and arrived there the same day, before a fortress named Colombo. On ditto there came four *Pangaeyen*, two of which were brought to the admiral and which were free men from Bengalen, who were allowed to sail unharmed, the other two stranded, which were unfree, both Portuguese, from which our people fished a lot of cotton cloths out of the breakers, but most drove on shore with the sea, as the foists went to pieces immediately".

12 The next entry in van der Hagen's journal as printed is the one of 31st December that follows this, no explanation being given of the *hiatus*. Craen's diary has the following :—" 22nd November. It was resolved to sail close before the castle of Colombo and each in passing to shoot and to sail on our course : on this fortress were only two guns (! ?), one should have been able to capture it with two ships. (In the account of this voyage in de Bry, 1606, we are told that from Cochin the ships directed their course to Zeylon, where they arrived the 22 ditto (November) and anchored near the town of Columba, where they fired some shots at the castle which answered with a shot at each ship.") From this island Selon comes (*sic*) the best pipes of cinnamon thence ; it is a beautiful land.—23rd November. A north-east wind, our course to east south-east ; at mid-day southern sun, the altitude of about 6 degrees. Selon, to wit Colombo, lies 6 degrees 50 minutes north of the line." From the same diary we learn that on 11th December it was resolved that the *Delft* with the Achinese ambassadors (*sic.*) but actually only the one surviving envoy and suite,) should leave the fleet and proceed direct to Achin. This took place next day, after a farewell banquet on the admiral's ship

13 This was one of the two ships sent to Mauritius.

King of Calicuth, that night[14], when he was with him warned him so often that he should not touch at Ceylon with his fleet, saying that there was not much of importance to the Hollanders in that country, and that he should pursue his voyage without touching at Ceylon[15]. And that (neither) the Samorijn nor anyone of his people had never[16]....given the admiral to understand of the murder that had taken place in Ceylon, he seems to have kept it concealed and secret, because he wished to speak with the admiral himself verbally, as he thought that had the admiral known of that he would not have got him on land so easily.

14 Of 11th-12th November, (see Craen's diary, s.d.).
15 Craen reports nothing of this.
16 *Sic.* In the document as printed there are dots (.. .) after this word, but no omission is apparent.

LETTER FROM THE KING OF SPAIN TO THE VICEROY OF INDIA, DATED 26th FEBRUARY, 1605.[1]

Dom Martim Affonso de Castro[2], friend viceroy, I the King send you all greeting. By letters from Ayres de Saldanha, the archbishop primate, the bishop of Cochin, and others that I received by the ships of the past year, I had advice of the disasters that had taken place in the conquest of Ceilam[3], and of how, after Dom Hieronymo de Azevedo had brought it into a good condition, all the black troops that he had in his army rebelled against him, excepting only Dom Fernando *modiliar*[4], with a thousand men of his following; from which resulted the rebel Dom Joao's recovering forces and courage with these troops that deserted to him, and capturing some forts with the garrisons of Portuguese that were in them, and chastising them and keeping them with him; and that after having made himself master of all this, he sent to the said Ayres de Saldanha ambassadors, asking of him terms of peace[5], and offering to return to our holy faith and my obedience[6]. on their being given to him a son of his[7],

---

1. This letter is printed in *Documentos Remittidos da India*, i. 8-11.
2. Left Lisbon, 2nd May, 1604, arrived at Goa, 19th May, 1605. (see *Arch. Port.-Or.* I. ii. 141-2), and succeeded Ayres de Saldanha as viceroy.
3. Details of these "disasters" are wanting: but P. du Jarrie, in his *Histoire des Indes Orientales*, ii. 795, says that on Candlemas day, (2nd Feb.), 1603, D. Jeronymo de Azevedo captured Balane (*cf. C. Lit. Reg. vi.* 334), and occupied it for four or five days, but had then, on account of D. Joãs's revolt (*sic.*), to retreat by way of Malvana to Columbo. Bocarro twice (45 and 508) refers to this retirement of D. Jeronymo's forces, and says that it was called "the famous retreat" (*a famosa retirada*). It is probable also that it is this affair that Baldaeus describes briefly in chap. v. of his *Ceylon*, and of which H. A. van Rheede speaks (Valentyn, *Ceylon* 265). See also Bree's journal, supra, under 13th May, 1603.
4. Regarding this man (the Samarakonràla of the Ràjàvaliya 99), see M. *Lit. Reg.* iv. 165 n.)
5. I can find no other reference to this embassy.
6. If Vimaladharma really made such an offer, we cannot believe that he intended to fulfil it.
7. This son, who is also referred to by Ryckx (see his journal supra, under 2nd June, 1603), must I think, have been born to Dom João when he was a professed Christian, the mother being his first wife, the daughter of Tammitaràla or Udammitaràla, (see supra, B. 1, note 35).

who is in that city of Goa in the college of the Kings[8], the which the said Ayres de Saldanha did not grant, and sent back the said ambassadors to Dom Hieronymo.

And that whilst the said rebel Dom Joao had despatched these ambassadors there arrived at Baticalou seven Dutch-ships[9], and in that latitude captured four Portuguese (ships[10]), and on Dom Joao's coming thither in order to confederate with them it did not effectuate, on account of dissentions that they had[11], although it appeared that in the end they were reconciled, and with a promise of being bound to return against the port and fortress of Gale[12]

From all these events I received the displeasure that you can consider, to see so greatly retarded the business of this conquest, which has cost so much trouble and blood of my vassals, in addition to the great expenses that for many years have been laid out on this part. And although the said Ayres de Saldanha advised that some forts had been recovered, and others had been fortified anew, and that on a ship's going direct from this kingdom to that island with men and munitions, the loss would be recovered, and it would be possible quickly to finish this conquest; nevertheless, considering the great need there is of going in aid with all the power of this State, and with that which can be sent from there to the ports of the South[13], in order to expel from them the rebels[14], as in another I advise you[15]; and taking in this the opinion of persons that understand it well, I have resolved to command to desist for the present from this conquest in the form in which it has hitherto been prosecuted; and that

---

8. The Franciscan college of the *Reys Magos* (Magi) in Bardez, where the scions of Asiatic royal families were educated. There were several Sinhalese lads there at this time (see infra, note 17).

9. The fleet of de Weert, which arrived at Matecalo on 25th April, 1603.

10. See the journals of Bree and Rycks under 16th-23rd May, 1603.

11. It is very strange that not a word is said of the massacre of de Weert and his companions.

12. This is hardly a correct statement of the fact.

13. "The South" was the term used by the Portuguese to denote what we call Malaysia.

14. The Dutch.

15. This letter does not appear in *Doc. Rem.*

the fortress of Columbo, with some other forts around that shall seem well to you, be fortified and conserved and that in them be placed the garrisons needful for their not being captured by the enemy; and that the fortress of Gale be likewise finished fortifying, in such manner that it may become defensible, and that in it be put the garrison of men, arms and munitions that shall seem necessary, in order to keep such good guard as befits a stronghold so important for the navigation of the South, and that it may not come into the possession of the enemies, who could from there (if they occupied it) do much harm to the navigation of the South, because of all the ship's sighting that point that come from those parts to India[16].

And in case the treaty of peace with the rebel Dom João be made in the future, or it appear to you that it can be concluded with good conditions, you shall effectuate it, securing yourself very well from the inconstancy and faithlessness of that people; and you shall propose in council whether for the greater security of the said terms of peace or in order to make war on the said rebel and expel him altogether from the island, it would be convenient to send to it the lad Dom Joao, grandson of Raju[17], who is being educated in the said college of the Kings, to whom the kingdom belongs[18], and give him some assistance with the least expense possible; and what you shall resolve thereupon as being most convenient you shall cause to be put into execution[19].

Written in Lisbon, the 26th of February, 1605.

THE KING....—FERNAO TELLER.

---

16. Cf. Sebald de Weert's letter supra, and note 58 there.

17. "Dom João" here is a mistake for "Dom Filippe" (as he is called in other letters in the *Doc. Rem.*); and the lad was in reality not grandson, but grand-nephew of Ràja Sinha's (see C. A. S. Jl. XX., 396, 398, 392 n. 5).

18. The Portuguese had maintained the right of Dona Catharina as heiress to the throne of Ceylon until she was captured by Konappu Bàndàra and forcibly made his wife; after which they transferred the right to the two captive youths D. João of Kandy and D. Filippe of Sittàvaka.

19. This proposal was not carried out, since Vimaladharma was already dead when this letter was written, and D. Filippe died a few years later.

LETTER FROM CAPTAIN ANTONIO MARTINS TO THE KING OF SPAIN, WRITTEN IN 1611, OR 1612.[1]

And as it appears to me very necessary to give your Majesty first a description of the island of Ceilão, which is that which the Dutch enemies aim at taking, and where I have been and served your Majesty many years, and where I have been a captive of the Moorish[2] Kings, with whom the said Hollanders have endeavoured to ally themselves, to treat of it becomes of the utmost importance and necessity, because thus with more light the malice of the enemy can be remedied and prevented, and it is as follows.

And besides the King of this island has on the coast thereof, towards the South[3], three ports, where he loads and discharges his goods ; one of them is called the port of Baticaloa, which is 70 leagues from our Point of Gale ; and further on, 14 or 15 leagues, he has another, which is called Triquilumaleque (*sic.*) ; and another further on, which they call the port of Cutiare.[4]

And I tell your Majesty that this said island of Ceilão is the key of the whole of India, in so far as concerns trade and merchandise, which is what aggrandizes and enriches it ; because all the ships that come from China, Japão, Malaca, Pegu, Bengala and the Malucas islands, and from the other

---

1. Of this letter (which was printed in *Doc. Rem.* iii. 100-13). I gave a complete translation, with introduction and notes, in the *M. Lit. Reg.* iv. 164-8. to which I would refer the reader. The importance of the letter in the present connection lies in the fact that the writer was (or professes to have been) an eye-witness of the massacre of de Weert and his companions.

2. Below the writer describes Vimaladharma as a " Moor.' The term is of course quite incorrect as applied to the Sinhalese. (For a similar error see C. A. S. Jl., xx. 232 et seq.).

3 In the Portuguese maps Batecalou is shown on the south coast. This writer goes further in placing Trincomalee also there.

4 The above confirms the statement of Davis (see Introduction) that trade by sea was carried on not only at Matecalo but at Trincomalee. The figures given for the distance between Galle and Matecalo are about right, if we reckon the league as equal to 3 miles, but as a fact the Portuguese league was about 4½ English miles. The distance between Matecalo and Trincomalee is absurdly understated. It will be noticed also that the writer locates Kottiyar beyond Trincomalee.

parts and regions of the South,[5] all of them by force of necessity are unable to reach India, unless they first manage to get a sight of and reach the said Point of Gale, in order that thus they may make a good voyage ; nor as little can the ships that sail from India for the said ports of the South neglect to get a sight of the said point.[6]

All this being then the truth, as it is, it is clear that if the said Dutch enemies were masters of this said island, or of its Point of Gale, which God forbid, with great ease they would become masters of all the ships that called there ; and the trade of India would infallibly be lost: and thus if Your Majesty does not command that this matter be taken up and remedied shortly, the said enemies will be masters of this country so fertile and so extremely valuable, and will very seriously injure the whole of India and its commerce, which may God forbid.

And in order that your Majesty may be pleased with the more diligence and speed to send and take measures against the pretensions and evil designs of these astute enemies, I may say that in the year (1) 603, in the time of the Moorish King who through arrogance called himself Dom Joao d'Austria,[7] the Hollanders arrived at the port of Baticalou, which is a port of the said Moor's as has already been said, and having entered with many kinds of merchandise, the said King came to receive them near the said port, and with great rejoicing on each side peace and perpetual friendship was agreed to between them, and to expel from the country the Portuguese that dwelt in it, vassals of your Majesty's, and thus they made a treaty[8] in the following manner.

---

5. The Portuguese always spoke of the countries beyond Ceylon as "the South."

6. Cf. supra, C. I. note 101.

7. The accusation is unwarranted, since the name of "Dom João d'Austria" was bestowed upon Konappu Bandara at his baptism by the Portuguese themselves.

8. No treaty seems actually to have been made (cf. the narratives of Bree and Rÿcks supra) ; but the writer states very accurately the requests of the Dutch and the promises of the King.

To wit: That the Hollander should be obliged to aid him by sea against the said Portuguese, and that by land he should do the same, without resting, until not one remained; and that when they had been expelled, the said Moor undertook to give them all the said three ports, which they (the Portuguese) now possess[9], and thus as they captured any one of them, the said Hollanders should become masters of it; and that he would also give them all the lading of pepper, cinnamon, and all the other commodities that might be in the island, and victuals and supplies for their ships, with other advantages besides.

And the treaty and confederation being celebrated with a great banquet,[10] which the King ordered for them and in my presence gave them, the supreme goodness of our Lord God permitted that the Dutch Governor ordered wine to be brought from his ships for the banquet, [11]and with it he gave a toast to the Moor,[12] who took it so much as an affront, that incontinently with great wrath he commanded him to be killed and all his men that were at the feast [13]; and thus their desire and pretension succeeded badly, and with sad lamentation the ships made their escape from the port,[14] wherefore this agreement did not take effect for the time being.

---

9. Columbo, Galle and Mature.
10. The purpose of the banquet was not what the writer states.
11. This writer is the only one that mentions this circumstance, which I see no reason to doubt.
12. The terms of the alleged toast are not given; but compare what Baldaeus says (infra F. 5) of the gross insult offered by de Weert to the King.
13. A great many more than those that were at the feast were killed.
14. A decidedly inaccurate version of the fact, seeing that the Dutch did not leave Matecalo roadstead until nearly two months after the massacre.

"THE VOYAGE OF FRANCOIS PYRARD" II., 146-7.[1]

This King [" Don Jouan "], having revolted and abjured the faith, put to death all the Portuguese that were found in his borders, and so it was that afterwards the Hollanders passing the *pointe de Galla* with three ships, as their wont is to cast anchor and make a sojourn there, contracted a peace and alliance with this King,[2] and such was the confidence reposed in one another, that the Hollanders used to go ashore in all freedom and assurance, and the Cingalla in like manner used to come aboard their ships. But upon this the King conceived a great treachery, assembling all the chiefs, principal soldiers, and most eminent men at his palace for a grand solemn banquet,[3] which he gave to all the highest grandees of his court and of the Nairs.[4] The Hollander general went thither in good faith with sixty or seventy of the chiefmen of his three ships,[5] chosen by himself, and arrayed in the bravest style possible. They were there received very magnificently, according to the custom of the country ; but the poor Hollanders' dessert was after another fashion, for while they were at table thinking only to enjoy themselves and make good cheer, they were incontinently seized and massacred there, and then by suborned villains.[6] The design of the King was at once to surprise all the ships, but God did not permit that, and saved them : for three or four mariners that were there waiting upon them escaped, and ran and flung

1. I quote from Mr. Albert Gray's admirable translation, as printed by the Hakluyt Society. Pyrard seems to have called at Ceylon on his way to Malacca in 1608 : his description of the island and of events there is full of inaccuracies, and the account he gives of the visit and massacre of de Weert is ludicrously erroneous.

2. This refers to Spilbergen's visit in 1602.

3. Here the writer proceeds to mix up de Weert's second visit to Ceylon in 1603, with the visit of Spilbergen in 1602.

4. The use here of this last word is of course absurd, there being no Nairs in Ceylon. Mr. Gray says that Pyrard's informants " meant probably the Tamils of Batticaloa," which may be correct, but Pyrard himself may be responsible for the blunder.

5. Spilbergen had only two ships ; de Weert had three on his first visit in 1602, but seven on his second visit in 1603.

6. There was no subornation in the affair, which was entirely unpremeditated and unexpected.

themselves into their boats, to give word to those on board the ships of what had taken place. So it was they straightway cut the cables, leaving their anchors there, laying a course for Achen, whither God conducted them, for all their pilots had been slain.[7] I have heard it said by the two Hollanders who came to the Maldives, and subsequently by others, that that general was one of the bravest and most valiant men that had come out of Holland this many a day, and that the rest of his comrades were of the same temper. The perfidious King that played them this sorry trick did it all to make his peace with the Portuguese ;[8] for I have heard them say themselves that this came about of their counsel, and that the King had promised to deliver up the ships to them, saving a part of the valuable cargo that he should retain.[9] The general was not slain at the time,[10] nor were two or three others ; but when the King saw that one part of his design had failed, he fell into such a rage and choler, that he had their eyes put out, and practised a thousand other cruelties upon them.[11] These Kings of Ceylon are sometimes friends, sometimes enemies, of the Portuguese, changing thus in a thousand fashions.

7. A very garbled version of the facts.
8. A most unjust allegation.
9. If the Portuguese made such a statement, it was a pure invention of theirs.
10. Amazing error.
11. Another slander.

MEMORANDUM ON CEYLON BY ADRIAN VAN DER MEYDEN, DATED, 20TH SEPTEMBER, 1660.[1]

Honorable sirs,—After King Emanuel of Portugal, A.D. 1497, through Vasco Gama had first discovered the East Indian route round the Cape of Hood Hope, and had occupied all the best harbours and bays, about a hundred years thereafter our united Netherlanders also came here to trade ; and the admiral Joris van Spilberghen arrived A.D. 1602 before Baticalo[2] and thereafter had speech with the Emperor of Candi about a quantity of pepper, and further with that prince regarding cinnamon, in order, if it was possible, to obtain them for a reasonable price, and then to come and fetch them from him yearly. The year after appeared here also the vice-admiral Sebalt de Weerd[3] with six[4] ships ; but he with fifty and odd[4] Netherlanders was (God better it) treacherously murdered on 1st May,[5] 1603 ; which his Majesty excused, because de Weerd also had wished to force him to come on board, or at least to the shore, in order to view his ships, or otherwise he would not help him to conquer Punto Gale ; although it was more probable that the Portuguese, with whom he was then again at peace, had arranged this thus for us, in order to expel us once for all from Ceylon[6]; although others lay the blame on the Emperor's envoy, [who had] come over from Atsjien with de Weerd,[7] and [had been] treated by him somewhat more contemptuously than the Portuguese ; who also think that in revenge for this insult, of having seated the Portuguese at the higher and him

---

1. This memorandum, addressed to the Governor-General and Council at Batavia by Adriaan van der Meyden on his retirement from the office of Governor of Ceylon in 1660, is printed in Valentyn's *Ceylon* 141-8, a portion of it (with verbal alterations) having already appeared in Baldaeus's *Ceylon*, chaps. xli.-xlii. (xlii.-xliii. of the English version).

2. No mention is made of de Weert's first visit to Ceylon.

3. Read " seven."

4. According to Rÿcks (supra) 47 men were killed and 6 mortally wounded.

5. Read " June."

6. An entirely unwarranted accusation.

7. No Sinhalese (but an Achinese) envoy accompanied de Weert ; and the statements that follow are probably pure inventions. (see further, infra, F2, note 5.

at the lower end at a meal, he had not only incited the Emperor against him [de Weerd], but had made the former believe that de Weerd plotted an attempt and treachery against the Emperor's life, and had no other reason than this for so earnestly inviting the Emperor on board his ships, and to the shore.

BALDAEUS'S "CEYLON." CHAP. VII.

After this came Sebald de Weert, vice-admiral to Wybrand van Warwjk, to Ceylon[1], and made a contract with the Emperor Don Jan,[2] proceeding on to Achin in order to collect a larger force, and arrived at Matecola with seven ships on 26th Aprll, A.D. 1603, and having informed the Emperor of his arrival, forthwith set out thitherwards[3], in order to speak with each other of the intended transaction. He then[4], having come to the vice-admiral Sebald de Weert at Matecola, asked in the first place after the captured Portuguese, taken from four vessels; and as the aforesaid de Weert had thoughtlessly released them, he exculpated himself in the matter, saying, that according to the engagement he could not hand them over; at which Don Jan was angry, and became suspicious, which suspicion was greatly increased by the ambassador of the Emperor, who had come with the vice-admiral Sebald de Weert from Achin[5], declaring that as

---

1. The English translator of Baldaeus erroneously makes Wybrand van Warwijk as well as de Weert come to Ceylon.

2. No contract was actually make between de Weert and Vimaladharma.

3. That is, to the town of Matecalo which was some miles from the roadstead (see the statements of Bree and Rÿcks.)

4. Valentyn (*Ceylon* 107-9) takes over, without acknowlegement, all that follows, altering the wording here and there, and introducing some statements from the Spilbergen journal or of his own.

5. Baldaeus appears to have copied this fiction about a Sinhalese envoy from the memorandum of Adriaan van der Meyden quoted above, and to have enriched it, in his usual style, with a number of details of his own invention. How van der Meyden came to transform the Achinese envoy into a Sinhalese, and whence he got the cock-and-bull story that he relates, I do not know: in any case, there is not the least ground for suspecting the Achinese envoy of playing a double part.

long as he was with the Hollanders he could perceive nothing else than that they were at one with the Portuguese, seeking by false means to deceive his Majesty, and to get possession of his country; that during the time of his ambassadorship he had not been paid respect to by the Hollanders, but on the contrary shamefully treated, causing, to the serious vilipendency of his imperial Majesty, whose person he represented, the Portuguese to sit at the upper end of the table, and him at the bottom, in addition releasing the aforesaid enemies, contrary to the promises given and the agreement made; from which could very well be guessed what was their intention. This envoy further testified that he had heard that the vice-admiral would invite the Emperor and the chief lords to view the ships, and manifest great signs of pleasure, in order thus to get his Majesty into his hands, and to invade the country: of which, as he was assured of it, he wished to warn his imperial Majesty, with the request that he would neither believe nor trust the Hollanders, so that his person with his princes and lords might not be betrayed, the territories laid waste, and the commonalty brought into slavery; protesting that he had quitted himself like a faithful servant of his master's, and a maintainer of the country's welfare, so that afterwards could not be laid to his charge the calamities that were at hand:— at this falling at the Emperor's feet, doing according to the manner of the country *sambaye*[6] or reverence.

Don Jan having heard this speech consulted with his lords as to what was to be done in this matter, seeing that the statement of the ambassador's appeared in part true, since the vice-admiral Sebald de Weert had plainly broken his promises in the release of the Portuguese; questioning whether

6. Baldaeus here, as in other places in his book introduces this word in order to display his knowledge. In the list of "Malay, Ambonese and other unintelligible words" prefixed to Valentyn's description of the Moluccas, *sombayen* is entered as a Malay word, and is explained as meaning "to bow down low reverentially with the hands above the head." The Portuguese adopted the word into their language in the form *Zumbaya*. It is Malay *sembahyang*, worship, ritual, prayer, which is a compound of *sembah*, a salutation, a respectful offering or address, the act of solutation or homage consisting in raising the hands to the face, and *yang*, divinity. The word *sembah* perhaps Sanskrit *sambhdvana*, worship, honour, respect, esteem.

MÁLE ISLAND

ROYAL PROCESSION TO "HUKURU MISKIT"

further trust should be put in him, or all further dealings broken off: upon which after various deliberations it was resolved that they should endeavour by all means to get the vice-admiral de Weert to go to Gale, in order according to the contract to invest the place, and meantime to notice how he de Weert should in that siege bear himself towards the Portuguese.

Sebald de Weert, having come to the Emperor, after many and various discussions begged and invited his Majesty to view the ships, which his Majesty declined, saying that his lords would not listen to it and that there was no reason to request it. Sebald, seeing that the King was not minded to come on board the ships, begged that his Majesty would just come to the shore and see the ships from afar; [saying] that to this end he had caused a tent to be bedecked with cloth, in order to lodge his Majesty therein. This was likewise refused, and gave the Emperor further suspicions; the aforesaid ambassador, who availed himself of this opportunity, and was prepossessed with great hatred against the vice-admiral because of the release of the Portuguese, and the slight done to him, saying: " See you [not], my most gracious lord, that my statement is true? because he seeks to get your Majesty into the net; therefore be on your guard;" with other assertions, all intended to strengthen still more the Emperor's suspicions.

The vice-admiral Sebald de Weert, being discontented at this refusal, answered, " that if his Majesty did not desire to come to the shore or on board the ships, he would not help him against the Portuguese:" at which speech Don Jan was angry with the aforesaid de Weert, but restraining his wrath said that according to his promises he [de Weert] was to sail with his ships for Gale, and that he [the Emperor] must go up to Candy to the Empress,—who, as his half-brother[7].

7. Further on Baldaeus has " step-brother." The *Mahavaṁsa* (328) calls Senerat Vimaladharma's " younger brother," while the *Rájávaliya* (100) says that Senerat was " the son of his (Vimaladharma's younger sister" (*i.e.*, cousin). What the real relationship was, I do not know.

Çenuwieraat Adasciin had gone to the frontiers[8], was all alone,—whence he would make haste to follow with the whole force.

Sebald, having drunk rather more than was proper[9], indiscreetly gave answer, " that the Empress would not want for a man[10], and that he did not wish to go to Gale, or to fight against the Portuguese, before and until his imperial Majesty had viewed the ships, and had shown him such tokens of honour." Don Jan, who was a very hasty and fierce man, was by these words inflamed to increased anger, and raging with fury like a fire stood up in haste saying, " *Banda lapa mebal,*"[11]. that is, " Bind me that dog," upon which words the vice-admiral was seized by four nobelmen, who tried to pinion him ; but as he resisted, drawing his sword, making a great outcry in order to obtain help from his men (but these had, at the request of the Emperor, remained at the shore), Sebald de Weert was meanwhile seized from

8. Where Baldaeus got this information from, I cannot say: it may be pure invention. At any rate, we know from the Sinhalese historians that before his accession to the throne Senerat was a Buddhist monk hence Baldaeus's statement is very unlikely.

9. This is confirmed by the statements of Rijcks and Antonio Martins, supra.

10. Commenting on this, Valentyn (*Ceylon* 108) says: " The first part of his answer was an expression [of such a nature] that he could not have employed worse of a public trull or brothel-whore, and that he used nevertheless of the Empress." Philalethes (*History of Ceylon* 92), in translating from Valentyn, does not give the English of the above, but says : " The first part of this answer was a gross insult upon the character of the Empress," and adds in a footnote : " The Dutchman says, with more plainness than would suit the refinement of English ears," and then quotes Valentyn's comment in the original Dutch. Knighton, in his *History of Ceylon*, after speaking of Senerat as " her [Catharina's !] brother, and giving Baldaeus's words in a fuller form, appends in a foot-note (p. 254) the comment of Valentyn in the original, but exposes his ignorance of Dutch by adding " was his insulting expression " ! It is impossible to say if de Weert actually made use of any such words as those attributed to him by Baldaeus, though doubtless he was, especially when intoxicated, quite capable of doing so.

11. Correctly, " *Bendapalla me balla.*" But according to the Spilbergen diarist (supra) Vimaladharma spoke in *Portuguese*, and his order was, not " *Bind* this dog," but, " *Kill* this dog..." One cannot help suspecting that here [as elsewhere] Baldaeus is displaying his knowledge of Sinhalese. At any rate, Valentyn here throws him overboard, and reports the King as saying " Mara [*sic*] isto can."

behind[12], and his head cleft with a broad sword, so that he fell dead to the ground, the which however no one durst inform the Emperor of, except the prince of Ove[13].

Don Jan was very much disturbed at this, saying: "why did you not take him prisoner as I ordered you?" the which the prince declared had been made impossible by the drawing of his sword; whereupon Don Jan answered: "Well, since he is dead, kill the rest also so that they may enjoy a like reward with their master;" which also was immediately carried out, there remaining of the persons that were on land with the vice-admiral only a youth, Isack Plevier of Vlissingen, whom the Emperor kept by him, and who was in his service on 22nd November, 1614[14], besides several that saved their lives by swimming to the ships...

The Emperor, after this deed had been carried out, returned to Candy, sending a short letter to the commanders of the ships, with these few words in Portuguese[16]. "*Que bebem vinho noa he bon. Devs fes justicia. Se quisieres pas, pas; se quires guerra, guerra.*" That is: "He who drinks wine is not good, and therefore God has done justice; consequently, if you desire peace, I give you peace; if war, war."[17]

---

12. Valentyn, evidently having before him the very realistic but entirely fanciful picture of the massacre in Baldaeus's book, adds "by a lock of hair."

13. Who this "Prince of Uva" was, I do not know. In the next chapter we read of his being murdered by Senerat, whose rival for the throne he was.

14. This Isaak Plevier is referred to in letters from Kandy by Boshouwer and Gÿsbert van Zuylen written from ten to fifteen years after the massacre of de Weert, and a letter sent to the Dutch at Matecalo in March, 1610, on behalf of the King of Kandy is signed "By me Isaac Ploviers of Vlissingen of the ship on which Lauwerims [*sic*] Franssen was captain." The mention by Baldaeus of the date "22nd November, 1614" is puzzling, but I suspect that it was the day of Plevier's death, since Gijsbert van Zuylem, in a letter from "Venoer," dated, 15th March, 1615, says:—"You must also be apprised of the death of Isaac Plauwiersz, who died some four to six months ago." Valentyn, in copying from Baldaeus, omits this clause, which contains an erroneous statement, in that it was in Senerat's and not Vimaladharma's service that Plevier died. I cannot help thinking that is to some letter of Plevier's that Baldaeus is indebted for the details he gives.

15. This may be true, though neither Bree nor Rÿcks mentions any men as having swum off to the ships.

16. Cf. the statement of Bree supra.

17. Valentyn alters the Portuguese a little, and gives a more literal translation. I suspect the Portuguese is Baldaeus's, and not Vimaladharma's, as it is by no means correct. It should probably read:—*Quem bebe vinho não he bom. justiça. Se quizereis paz, paz; se quereis guerra, guerra.*"

Don Jan lived [but] a short time after Sebald's death[18], falling into a great sickness, having such unbearable burning within his body, that he had to lie constantly in cold water, without however obtaining in any wise relief therefrom. His drinking water was brought from a little river, named Halgradoje[19], lying between the districts of Ove and Matarette, which is so cold, that one can hardly take it into the mouth, but this water likewise could not cool his burning. He often lamented the Netherlanders that were struck dead innocently, but the vice-admiral Sebald de Weert, he said, "had well deserved it." During his illness he could never rest, nor settle any order in the Kingdom, and that through intolerable pain, which finally deprived him of life in the year 1604[20]. He left behind a son, named Mahastanne Adascijn, and two daughters, the one called Soria Mahadascijn, or "Well-beloved Sunshine," the other Cathan Adascijn, that is, "Well-beloved Peace," whom he had got by Dona Catharina, named in Cingaleese Mahabandige Adascijn, that is, "Well-beloved Empress."[21]

18. The account Baldaeus gives of Vimaladharma's last days is the only one that has come down to us [so far as I know], and it is probable that for these details we are indebted to Isaak Plevier.

19. The Halgranoya [which is crossed by the main road from Nuwara Eliya to Udapussellawa) is evidently the river referred to, and the location is fairly correct. Valentyn rather absurdly abbreviates this part as follows :—" so that he was constantly obliged to lie in water, that was so cold, that one could not keep it in the mouth."

20. It is unfortunate that the month and day are not given, as no other writer supplies these details. *The Rájáwaliya* says (100) that Vimaladharma died after a reign of 12 years in the hill-country," " in the year 1525 of the Saka era," *i.e., A.D.* 1603-4.

21. Spilbergen and de Weert [see supra] mention only one daughter and one son. On the other hand, the *Rajawaliya* says (98) :—" The Queen [Catharina] bore four sons and one daughter to Vimaladaham Súriya ; the names of the four princes were, his highness *(Ásthánaya)* Rájásuriya, his highness Udumále, his highness Kumarasinha, and his highness Vijeyapála," the daughter's name not being given, and states that when the King was dying he committed his " four sons " to the care of his cousin and successor. Baldaeus has taken his information from a Portuguese document written probably in 1643, which is printed in Judice Biker's *Collecção de Tratados, &c.* i. 218-25. This says :—" D. João died in the year 1604, leaving with D. Catharina his wife a son, called Mahastana, and two daughters, the elder Soria Mahadassin, and the younger Antanassin." (According to this authority Kumárasinha and Vijayapála were the sons of Senerat, and not of Vimaladharma). It is evident therefore that " Cathan' is an error : perhaps the ms. that Baldaeus copied from had Çãtan, *i.e.* Çantan. Valentyn has " Cathan, or Hantanne, and (according to another report Hatane (!) Adassyn."

"REBELION DE CEYLON." BY JOAO RODRIGUEZ DE SÁ EMENEZES, CAP X.[1]

Pledged by so many causes to this conquest, our princes continued it with various successes the whole time that the tyrannical reign of the rebel Don Juan, the mortal enemy of our nation, lasted; and prosperously enjoying the fruits of his tyranny, four years after the death of Pedro Lopes he obtained a considerable victory over the general D. Jeronimo de Azevado;[2] and his prosperity not stopping there, his almost insuperable arms outweighing our fortune, he gave entrance to the Hollanders in the year, 1601.[3] There having put into the port of Batecalou the general Jorge Aspielberg with three ships,[4] he brought them[5] to Candia, and welcomed them with applause and public rejoicing, assigning them a site where they might build a fortress and factory, in hatred of the Portuguese, and to flatter Maurice, from whom he had an embassy, and in respect of them he began to intitle Candia "new Flanders," [and] learnt the French[6] language with a view to gain over the heretics in order that they might aid him to expel our people from Ceylon. There has been printed in one volume[7] some ruttiers, written in the Latin and French languages, of these and other voyages that they made to Asia, so full of lies, that the least informed in the matters of the East could detect them; because they make it all their study and business to accuse the Spaniards, and speak evil of their valour, industry and religion.

The just indignation that obliged me to reply to the falsehoods with which these Calvinists provoke us must be

---

1 As the translation by Lt.-Col. St. George in the C.A.S. Jl. xi. 555-9 is in parts very incorrect, I have made a new translation from the original, published in 1681.

2 See supra, B1, note 101.

3 A misprint for 1602.

4 Spilbergen arrived with only one ship, another arriving later; the third did not come to Ceylon, but proceeded to Achin (see Introduction).

5 The Dutch.

6 An odd mistake for "Dutch" or "Flemish."

7 Apparently de Bry's publication is meant, though the description is inaccurate.

the apology for this short digression ; and returning to the barbarian[8] of Candia, the friendship and consideration that he contracted with them attained to great prosperity, although it is true that there did not at that time result from this league any harm to our people ; because it vanished through fears and distrusts of the Flemings, so that on the admiral Jacobo Necio's[9] returning the following year with some ships to the port of Batecalou, the King of Candia went from his court to see him, and the admiral disembarking to receive him with the best and finest from his armada, and wishing to force the King, in order to welcome him, to go on board his ships, by his excessive[10] persistency, he rendered the compliment suspicious ; wherefore the barbarian, estimating the mind of the heretic by his own so accustomed to treasons, taking apart him and his principal companions under colour of regaling them on land cut them all in pieces.[11] Thus did that apostate continue (*sic.*) the friendship of his greatest confederates, smirching the sacrosanct laws of hospitality so many times by sacrificing to his idols the blood of so many innocents, although in spite of his ill-deeds the Calvinists praise him in their writings as a great prince solely because of the inexorable[12] hatred that he displayed towards the Portuguese, although provoked by this wrong they never more dared trust in his word, though they dissembled the outrage ; because they are people with whom the convenience of the state has more force than the reputation of honour, and as they strove so much to enter into the island, they did not lose the means of obtaining it, seeking all that there were to render the Portuguese odious to the Zingalas in order to provoke them to our injury.[13]

---

8 Vimaladharma was in no sense a "barbarian," but a well educated and able statesman.

9 By "Jacobo Necio" is meant Jacob van Neck. The writer appears to have been misled by the erroneous reference to van Neck in the "address to the reader" prefixed to the Eighth Part of de Bry's collection (see supra, D2, introduction).

10 Or, "unmannerly."

11 Lt-Col. St. George (loc. cit. p. 558) has misinterpreted this passage in the most extraordinary manner.

12 The original has the impossible word "inexacrable."

13 The writer then records the prophecy referred to supra, D2, at note 41, which, he says, the Dutch utilized to their advantage.

DESCRIPTIONS OF THE SOUTH - EASTERN, SOUTHERN, AND SOUTH-WESTERN COASTS OF CEYLON AT THE END OF THE SIXTEENTH CENTURY.

(*From Linschoten's* "*Reys-Geschrift Uande Navigatien der Portugaloysers in Orienten,*" *&c.*. **1595**).[1]

CHAPTER II.

Deroute,[2] or the Navigation and course from India to Porto Piqueno de S. Iago,.....in the kingdom of Bengalen, &c.

Whoever wishes to sail from India to Porto Piqueno,[3] or the little Harbour, situated in Bengalen, to wit, outside of the island of Seylon, must set sail from the harbour of Cochijn from the 10th.[4] to the 20th of April, taking his course along the coast, as far as a place named Brinjao.[5] (which lies near the cape or point of Comorijn, to wit, the uttermost point or end of the Indian coast south-westwards), from there taking his course south, as far as $6\frac{2}{3}$ degrees, and from there south-east, as far as $5\frac{2}{3}$ degrees. On getting there you shall run east, until you have the island of Seylon in sight: because the point of Seylon, named *A ponta de Gualle,* (that is to say, "the point of the galley,"[6]) is the furthest land thereof lying in the south under the altitude of 6 degrees; so that, if one holds this course at $5\frac{2}{3}$ degrees, he cannot fail to have sight of the said island of Seylon. This way and course you shall

---

1. This is the second part of Linschoten's famous work, and appeared before the first part (see Hakluyt Society's edition of his *Voyage,* Introd. xxx). This second part was carried by all the earliest Dutch voyagers to the East, including Spilbergen (see supra, B1, note 8).

2. This word represents the Portuguese *derrota,* course. On Linschoten's fondness for using synonymous words in several languages see the Hak. Soc. ed. of his *Voyage,* Introd. xl.-xli.

3. Satganw on the right bank of the Húghli (see Hak. Soc. ed. of Linsch. i. 95, and *Hobson-Jobson* s. vv. 'Porto Piqueno Porto Grande').

4. By a printer's error, apparently, the English translation has "which" for "10th."

5. Read "Brinjão." See note 8 infra.

6. Linschoten repeats this absurd interpretation of the name several times.

thus hold, leaving Cochijn from the 13th to the 20th April, as before [said]: because if you depart from there later, you will need to be more on your guard, because then the winds begin to blow very strong from the south, having at other times the winds blowing very furious and turbulent from the south-west and north-west.

When you come to see this island of Seylon, you shall run along the coast there (one runs along the coast east and west and has somewhat of east by north and west by south) as far as the first shoal lying in 6 degrees scarce, and the other shoal lies still further in 6½ degrees, being separated from the other 7 miles),[7] in the same direction of east and west and east by north and west by south. From the point *A punta de Galle* to the first shoals is about 28 miles.

CHAPTER 12.

Another Description of the same Voyage and course... recorded by another pilot, more fully and correctly related, with all the situation and extent thereof.

Sailing from the coast of India to the harbour named Porto Piqueno in the kingdom of Bengalen, to wit, outside of the island of Seylon, you shall take your course along the coast of India, and will come to see Brinjao,[8] lying near the C. de Comorijn, the uttermost end of the coast of India, taking your way from there right across: because from here onward it is a good country and makes the shortest way across, as also to go assured of not falling inside of or between

---

7. It will be noticed that the figures for distances and degrees differ in the several ruttiers.

8. Vilinjam, 12 miles south of Trivandram in Travancore. It was burnt by D. Lourenço de Almeida in 1506 (see C. A. S. Jl. xx. 25). William Hore, who anchored here in March, 1619, calls the place, "Brimion," and Martin Pring, who spent several days there in April, 1618, spells the name "Brin Jan." Pring does not say anything of the dunes mentioned below but speaks of "a high picked hill like unto a sugar-loafe, bearing north-east by east by the compasse; which is the best marke if it be cleane, to know the place." (*Purchas his Pilgrimes*, v. 70, 6). In Dalrymple's collection of maps, plans and charts, (1774-92), vol. 5, is a view of "Brinhojn Hill" in 1701.

9. That is region of the sea (see *New Engl. Dict.* s.v. "Country, 1" q.v.) The orig. has "*contreye*."

the island of Seylon.[10] So when you come to see the *Barreiras*[11] that is, the dunes of Brinjaon aforesaid, you shall run south, taking your course thus far from 15 to 20 miles, and from there onwards you shall shorten your way, according as you think best and have opportunity, in order to come under 5 degrees; on getting there you shall run east as much as you think needful in order to assure yourself of being able to round the point or cape of Gualle, which is the uttermost end of the island of Seylon, at the south-west side, lying under the altitu of 6 degrees. When you think you are in the region of the *Punta de Galle*, in order to be surer, you shall approach the island so as to recognize it, before you come near the shoals, to wit, between Tanadare[12] (which is 5 miles from the Punta de Ġalle) and the first shoal, where in general all ships can recognize the land, of those that wish to sail to Bengalen.... Having the land in sight in the aforesaid country, approach it as close as you wish, only not passing under 12 fathoms towards the land, because there lie some rocks along shore, of which one has not particular knowledge, besides the shoals, between which and the land one may sail, as shall be said hereafter.

Sailing thus, as has been said, along the land, you must know that the land of Tanadare (in order to recognize the same), to wit, from there onwards 5 miles as far as the shoals on the shore of the sea, is altogether a low land. And when further on you begin to see inland some mountain ranges, to wit, 3 great mountains, on coming opposite to them you shall forthwith come to see the first shoal,[13] between which and the land one may well pass: because most of the ships that go and come past the island sail through there; you shall find there, to wit, midway between it and the land," to 12 fathoms depth good and in some places stony ground, and you have nothing else to fear there, but what you see

10. *Sic* in orig: "and the mainland" is understood.
11. Port., meaning "barriers," also "targets," or "butts." (compare the description of the south coast of Ceylon in chaps. 18 and 19 below).
12. Dondra
13. The Great Basses, or Bassas (Port. *baixos*, shoals) reef, regarding which see Imray's *Indian Ocean Pilot* 891-2.

before your eyes. This first shoal lies under the altitude of 6½ degrees full, and right opposite thereto you will see on land a single rocky hill,.[14] without seeing any others in all this region. From this first and great shoal 6 miles further on lies another but smaller shoal: [15] one sails from one to the other north-east and south-west, and has somewhat of north-east by east and south-west by west. This little shoal lies under 6¼ degrees, distant about two miles from the land: if you wish to sail through between it and the land you may well do it, because one has there 5 to 6 fathoms depth at low water with sandy ground, which I know from one who has passed through there more than thirty times, both in going and returning; but if one has a big ship, it is better to keep outside to seaward of it.

Having passed the aforesaid shoals you sail on along the land, without diverging therefrom, because it is a good course to sail forward close thereto; and on coming past the end [16] of the mountains and the high land,[17] you will come to see a high pointed top standing in amongst other mountains, from which projects a prominent peak sloping to the south-west: this top is named *O Capello de Frade,* that is, "the monk's cowl or hood"; [18] it is under the altitude of 8 degrees full. I do not put down here the course that one takes along this coast as far as the aforesaid *Capello de Frade,* because one does not sail along it in any direct course. This *Capello de Frade* forms a cape or point of land, from which runs a reef projecting half a mile to seaward on which one sees the water breaking in some places.[19] From this point as far as Trinquanamale is 17 miles: one runs along the coast north and south, which is everywhere low land having all along there a shelvy ground, and you will see none of the land except away inland.[20] 5 miles before one comes to

14. Probably the "Rocky Knob (resembling a square tower)" of modern charts, or, possibly, Little Elephant hill.

15. The Little Basses, or Bassas, reef, regarding which see Imray's *Ind. O. Pilot* 892-3.

16. The Eng trans. has the curious error "Iland" for "end."

18. The well-known Friar's Hood. (Cf. supra, B1, note 11, D3.) note 3).

19. This is an extraordinary error, the Friar's Hood being many miles inland.

20. By an error, the Eng. trans. has "inward five miles."

Trinquanamale one finds a little river.[21] Trinquanamale is a large harbour, having at the mouth more than 3 miles breadth; at the entrance thereof is low land, being everywhere deep: he that wishes to go in there to anchor may lie under the shelter of one of the islands; within is a river that runs as far as to Seyta Vagua;[22] as far as here[23] is everywhere low land. To recognize Trinquanamale from afar, it must be known that at the mouth thereof situated on the North side is a dune of yellowish colour, and it has on the one cape or point two far-stretching mountains of elevated land, extending right inland, without one's seeing before or afterwards any other high land besides along the sea-shore.

CHAPTER 18.

Deroute or the course of navigation from Malacca to Goa, with all the extent and situation thereof declared at large.

In the course to the island of Seylon you shall sail under 7½ and 7 degrees, with which course you shall come to the island of Seylon, to a place named Matecalou, which is to luffward of the shoals; here one has no ground but within 2 miles of the land. You must also be warned that from the middle of the gulf to the island of Seylon the currents and streams (in this season or *mouson*) run out to seaward; likewise the compass ever deviates more towards the north west, to which you shall always have good regard. And coming to the island of Seylon, on getting sight of it, you must not lose it again, always keeping bottom, to wit, from under 30 fathoms (looking well to yourself and guarding against the shoals, which are bad and perilous, the outermost thereof being of stone and rocks, the length of a galley, without having any more but what one sees). Running into the depth of 14 and 16 fathoms, at halfway or midway from

---

21. Perhaps the Virgil-ganga.

22. This river is, of course, the Mahaweli-ganga; but it cetrainly does not take its rise at Sitáwaka. The statement shows how ignorant the Portuguese were of the interior of Ceylon.

23. The Eng. trans., in place of these four words, has "the other to it."

there and the land you will find the aforesaid depths and another shoal that remains behind you, which is the first, and one can see nothing but that the sea breaks thereon; they say that with small ships one can pass between it and the land, being 4 fathoms in depth, notwithstanding it is better to keep to seaward thereof. From here to the land is a mile distant; you may approach it up to 16 and 18 fathoms, and if by chance you find yourself here at night, it will be needful to sail with the foresail only, to wit, when one has sight of unknown land, not passing under 18 fathoms towards the land, nor above 30 fathoms to seaward.

From this shoal onwards one must run along the coast, in depths of 15, 16, and 20, 25, 30 fathoms, but in such manner that you do not lose bottom; because you may have calms so that, losing bottom, the currents and streams might drive you to the island of Maldiva, wherefore it is needful to have a good lookout until one comes to Negumbo (which is in the island of Seylon), from whence it is good to run right across to the main land. On coming to Negumbo you shall not put off from the land, except from 15th February onwards: because from that time forward the currents and streams begin again to run inwards; and it being from 15th February onward you may sail away from the land (to wit, from the islet of Verberijn,[24] which lies close by the coast of Seylon, as far as the fortress of the Portuguese called Columbo)[25], as you shall best have opportunity, so that it may not befall you as it has happened with many ships, which through heedlessness have been driven to the islands of Maldiva.

From this last shoal to Tanadare and as far as the cape named *A Punta de Galle*, to wit, along the coast and seashore, the land is everywhere almost alike and equally high, and right opposite the aforesaid shoal one sees inland three high mountains. From here as far as Tanadare one has sandy shores; you may throughout run along the land without fear, as far as in sight of Tanadare, which is very well recognized, and let it not deceive you: because coming to it from without

24. Béruwala.
25. In the orig. the parenthesis mark is placed after "Seylon," but the sense seems to require it to be here.

it looks like the *Punta de Galle*. The signs and right indication thereof are as follows: to wit, it has a prominent point of narrow land, forming the fashion of a tongue, with a reef of stone projecting therefrom seaward, the length of a good stone wharf; this point of land or projecting tongue is full of Indian palm-trees, which present themselves very beautiful and charming to the view,[26] and a mile or two before one comes thereto this cape or point of land has the appearance of a tongue, to wit, outside the palm-trees towards the sea: but the grove of palm-trees in itself is thick and beautiful in appearance; and before one comes to Tanadare one has two or three sandy bays, whereof there is no need to make mention.

So when you come opposite to this grove of palm-trees, you will see in the middle of it a white *pagode* (that is, an Indian idol temple or idol);[27] from this *pagode* to the north side you will see some butts or dunes of white and red earth, which are good landmarks and the right indication of this region; you must not come too close to the land, because there is a small shoal projecting somewhat to seaward, but only a little; when you discover these aforesaid butts you shall sail into 18 and 20 fathoms depth: because if the wind begins to drop, and the bottom to become deeper, you shall cast anchor; because if you neglected that, you would soon be off the ground, because the currents and streams run very strongly to seaward.

From Tanadare to Belliguao is about 6 miles: this place Belliguao is a very large bay, and on the south side of it are seen some big butts or mounds of red earth,[28] to wit, inside in the bay: because one cannot see them except when one has completely discovered the bay; and on the north side it has two little islets close to the land, from which islets a small shoal projects · but it is from the south side towards the land.

---

26. The "Indian palm-trees" are, of course coconut trees, which grow densely on Dondra Head.

27. It is curious that the writer gives both meanings of the word (see *Jobson-Jobson* s.v. 'Pagoda').

28. An old name for Weligama Bay was "Red Bay," from the red cliffs seen from seaward.

From Belliguao to Gallee is 5 miles: this course from Belliguao to Gallee is altogether along the seashore full of palm-trees, and between both lies an Islet (close to the land) of rocks.[29]

So when you come near to Gallee you will come to see a high flat land full of woods, and a level wilderness, and on the north side of the bay it has a large grove of palm-trees; and if it were needful for you to anchor in the bay, you might well sail in up to 15 and 14 fathoms depth; but he that wishes to follow his course has no object in running in.

From Tanadare to this harbour of Gallee (which is 12 miles) one sails from the one to the other north-west and south-east and has somewhat of north-west by west and south-east by east. You must be warned not to make this course along this coast to Guallee without bottom.

From Guallee to the point named Belitote[30] is five or six miles, which point has a thick grove of palm-trees (and right opposite there about half a mile away it has a large rock), and between both lie many rocks along the land[31]. Near this point of Guallee lie two shoals on which water breaks: one lies before one comes to the point, which projects ¼ mile to seaward, and the other right opposite to the bay, projecting a little mile to seaward on the north side; and against these you must principally guard yourself[32]. One may well sail past here in the night, having conveniently 20 fathoms depth, so there is nothing to fear. On this shoal[33] the sea breaks sometimes very gently, to wit, when it is high tide.

All along from here one may take his course to Columbo, just as the coast extends, and from the island of Verberijn onward the bottom is shelvier or shallower.

On coming close to Columbo, to wit, at 3 or 4 miles towards near Negumbo,[34] one may everywhere anchor in 8 or

---

29. I do not know what islet is referred to.

30. Welitota.

31. The Eng. trans. has "many stonie cliffes: along the shore, by the point of Gualle, are two sandes."

32. The first "shoal" is probably the Outer Kadda Rocks, and the other, one of the numerous rocks with which Galle Harbour abounds.

33. The Eng. trans. has "same," a misprint, apparently, for "sande"

34. This is expressed rather oddly, and I am uncertain of the writer's exact meaning.

9 fathoms : but near Columbo you must not do it, unless it were of great necessity, then you might anchor within 18 fathoms of the land. One has there stony bottom, and the same is the case also above 25 fathoms to seaward, and that in most places. You must everywhere be on your guard when you cast anchor to prove that first with the lead : the bottom of this region is in some places small and in other coarse sand, which is the safest ; there is also occasionally red sand ; likewise patches of white and black sand. These are the signs of the bottoms along this coast, on all of which bottoms one may anchor.

The proper marks and indication of Columbo (which is where the Portuguese have their fortress) are these : to wit, when one is in the harbour, the so-called *Pico* of Adam (which is a high peak, the highest of all the surrounding region) will be in the east. Making your course towards the harbour of this fortress, you will gradually come to lose all the mountains and hills, and begin to come near thin[35] or flat low land, which is a sign of the harbour and a very good indication.

The winds that one will find here mostly at this season or *monson* will be north-north-east, north-east and sometimes east-west-east and also east winds. The *viraçoins* (that is, the winds that blow from the sea) are often in the north and north-west. I make this explanation, in order that no one may be surprised at finding such there. In like manner one finds there also even west-north-west, west and west-south-west winds, according to the conjunction of the season when one comes to that coast. These winds, which are called *viraçoins*, which generally blow from out of the west through the whole of India, to wit, the time that one spends at sea (which is in the summer from the afternoon to midnight), come from the sea to the land, wherefore they are named by the Portuguese *viraçoins*[36], that is to say, winds from the sea. But from midnight on to midday the winds generally blow from out of the east, which come from across the land

35. That is, thinly wooded.
36. Port. *viraçoes*, plural of *viração*, breeze (from *virar*, to turn, to *bear*).

to the sea, called by the Portuguese *terreinhos*[37], that is to say, winds from across the land to the sea : as we have explained more fully touching all this in my *Itinerario* and description of India [38]; it is only related here so that it may appear strange to no one, the manner of the description of it, and the blowing of the winds along all this coast. When you wish to set sail by night with the *terreinhos* (or land-winds), if they are not north-east you must not set sail but from midnight onwards ; and if they do not veer[39] (blowing seaward) you must not put off too far from the land, because it would be difficult for you to sail far to seaward, in order afterwards to come again to the land, because the *viraçoins* or sea-winds from the north and north-west often come slowly and feebly.

CHAPTER 19.

Description of all the Harbours, Places, Coasts and Shoals on the east and south sides of the Island of Seylon with their altitudes, courses, extent and the situation thereof, with the navigation all along there, as far as the fortress of Columbo, where the Portuguese have their residence.

In the first place, beginning from Trinquanamale, which lies under the altitude of 9 degrees, to wit on the east side of the island of Seylon : 8 miles south from here lies a small river[40], and before one comes to this river, coming from Triquanamale, there are some islands[41] (which are whitish from bird's dung). At the mouth of this aforesaid river also lie two little islets[42], which are full of trees. From Triquanamale to this river the course is north and south and north by east and south by west. Running along the coast to this river, you must leave the aforesaid islands on the land side, going outside of them : because between them and the land

---

37. Port. *terrenho*, earthen, land (adj.) : hence land-wind, *vento* being understood. (See *Hobson-Jobson* s.v. 'Landwind')
38. See Hak. Soc. ed. of Linsch. i. 234.
39. The Eng. trans. has "if they be not full."
40. See note 21 supra.
41. I cannot identify these.
42. I cannot identify these.

are many stones, and rocks. This river and Trinquanamale lie about 8 or 9 miles the one from the other, as before (said)[43]

From the aforesaid river (with the islands at the mouth or entrance) to the river of Mataqualou[44] is 12 miles, and it lies under the altitude of 7⅛ degrees ; the course from the one to the other is north-west and south-east. This river being passed, coming between the islands and into[45] the mouth, you may approach the land as near as you will : because it is everywhere good and clear. At a pederero [46] shot from the land one runs into 20 fathoms depth.

From Matecalou to about 5 or 6 miles away, the course is north and south as far as a point or cape. From this point other 5 or 6 miles onward one runs along the coast north and south and north by east and south by west. Somewhat further on towards the first shoals, as far as about 5 or 6 miles to the north, stands a grove of palm-trees ;[47] on coming opposite thereto one runs along this coast north-north-east and south-south-west and somewhat north by east and south by west. From this five miles towards the first shoal the course is north-east and south-west and north-east by east and south-west by west. Before one comes within 4 or 5 miles of this shoal you will see some hills and heights of red earth, to wit, along the sea-coast near the shore, and inland are visible some high mountains, and the most northerly of all of these mountains has a hillock projecting above, which appears to be a blockhouse[48], and is of red earth. One may sail through between this first shoal and the land in 7 and 8 fathoms depth, to wit, as far from the shoal as from the land : because from there to the land is a mile away ; and in sailing around outside to seaward you will find everywhere sandy bottom. This aforesaid shoal lies under the altitude of 6 degrees.

---

43. The Eng. trans. has, instead of these last words, " at the furthest."

44. There was no " river of Mataqualou," as Spilbergen discovered (see supra, B1, note 8).

45. This word appears to have got in by a printer's error.

46. Orig. " *guetelingh*." The Eng. trans. has " a great shotte."

47. Cf. supra, B1, note 10.

48. Perhaps, Westminster Abbey is meant. The maps in the Spilbergen journal gives a mountain that seems to be intended for this, with a " blochuis " near the foot.

About 6 or 7 miles south of this shoal there is yet another shoal, and from the one to the other one runs along the coast east-north-east and west-north-west. This second shoal lies under the altitude of scarce 6 degrees, between which and the mainland there are 12 to 13 fathoms depth, all clear bottom.

From this last shoal to a bay named Ajalla[49] one runs along the coast east and west and east by north and west by south.

Four or 5 miles further on from this bay of Ajalla lies another bay, named Ilulpulam[50], from whence to Tanadare may be 7 miles.

Tanadare is a point of land, on which stands a grove of palm-trees, and when one comes right opposite here one will come to see a white *pagode* (that is, an Indian idol temple); and on the north side of this pagode stand some butts or mounds of white and red earth. Sailing past here, you must not come very close to the land : because some shoals lie there. This point being passed, you straightway run into 20 fathoms depth : because everywhere it is good and clear bottom, and if the wind failed you it is good anchoring there.

From Tanadare to Belliguon is about 6 miles. Belliguon is a very large bay, having on the south side some large hillocks of red earth, which stand inside in the bay: because one cannot see them before and until one has wholly discovered the bay ; and on the northside there are two islets lying close to the land ; along these islets runs a reef or shoal from the south side thereof.

From Belliguon to Gualle is 5 miles. On this course from the one to the other the land is everywhere dense and full of palm-trees, to wit, right along the sea-coast. About half way, from Belliguon to Gualle lies a rocky islet close to the land, and yet another on the south side of Gualle ; in sailing towards it, you will see a high flat land, full of trees, and of a level wilderness ; and on the north side of the bay there stands a large grove of palm-trees, on the edge of the sea ; and inside the harbour you will see a white house, which is a churchlet

49. Cf. supra, B1, note 141.
50. Cf. supra, B1, note 141.

of our dear Lady..[51] Sailing from Belliguon to Gualle (and coming opposite to this point) on the south side towards the bay, you shall take care to put to seaward, in order to avoid a shoal whereon one sees the water break; and in order to anchor, you must run to north and north-north-west, in such wise that you continually have open some rocks (which stand on the north side), and inwards of the bay you shall see the grove of the palm-trees, the which will be on the south side of you towards Belliguon, which is hidden from you by the point, you will there find 14 ot 15 fathoms depth, and running as far as 13 fathoms, and finding sandy bottom, you shall anchor: because to seaward is everywhere rock.

From Tanadare to this harbour of Gualle (which is 12 miles) one runs from one to the other north-west and south-east and north-west by west and south east by east. This harbour of Gualle lies in 5⅓ degrees.

Following the coast around from Gualle sailing towards the fortress of the Portuguese (named, Columbo).[52] This course and navigation we have sufficiently set forth in detail in the Navigation of Malacca to India, wherefore it is not necessary to relate it again.

51. The Eng. trans has "a small chappell of the Virgin Marie."
52. The sentence stands thus in the orig.

THE BATTICALOA AND PANAWA TERRITORIES: AS DESCRIBED BY GOVERNOR RJKLOF VAN GOENS IN OCTOBER, 1675.[1]

Going somewhat further[2]. we come now to the jurisdiction of the territories of Batticalo, that have their beginning in the north, with the aforesaid river of Nateoer[3], or the inlet of Venlo's Bay[4], and ending in the south with the gravet of Samgam Candi[5], making along the seaboard at the very least a distance of 16 German miles[6], or for an ordinary pedestriaan 24 hours' journey, and to landward, where this territory ends at the confines of the Weddas, 5, 6, 7, 8, and 9 hours' journey, and used of old to be ruled by special *bandares*, descended from the aforesaid three-breasted woman and the Tanasserysh prince[7]; but afterwards, owing to mutual disagreements and wars, conquered by the Malabaarish and Jaffanapatnamish Kings, derived from the same stock, as has been already herebefore in some measure related, and who still held sovereign rule about the year 1500, before the arrival of the Portuguese, in such wise that the Candian King never after that had

---

1. I translate this from the description of Ceylon, &c. written by Rjklof van Goens the elder, on vacating the governorship of Ceylon, for presentation to the Governor-General and Council at Batavia, and dated at that place 24th September ,1675. This extremely valuable document, the original of which has unhappily disappeared, was printed (in an abbreviated form unfortunately) by Valentyn in his *Ceylon* 204-46,. and the passage here translated occurs on pp. 222-6

2. The writer has been describing the district of Tambancarrewarre (Tamankadawara now Kòralai Pattu), and is now going southward.

3. The Nàttúr river is a branch of the Maduru-oya, which disembogues at Válaichchénai. In the map of Ceylon in the *History of Ceylon* by "Philalethes" the point north of "Natoor River" is called "Point Oude Grens" the last two words meaning in Dutch "old limit."

4. This bay was named either from the town of Venlo (in Limburg), or, more probably, from a ship bearing that name, which, may be, was the first to visit it after the Dutch obtained a footing on Ceylon, (Cf. *C. Lit. Reg.* ii. 351, C. A. S. Jl. xvii. 318). On English maps the name appears in all kinds of erroneous forms, such as Vendeloos, deloos, Vánderloos, &c.

5. Sengamámkanda, a little north of Kómariya.

6. By the present coast road the distance is about 80 miles.

7. In the earlier part of his report van Goens gives the legendary origin of the Sinhalese, falling into the same error as that committed by Couto (V. I. v.) in making Vijaya come from Tenasserim. The "three-breasted woman" is Kuvéni (see *Rájáwaliya* 18).

complete rule over them, but had to content himself yearly with some presents of wax, honey and other trifles[8].

The Portuguese also were never able to obtain further jurisdiction than over the islet of Poelian[9],. where they used to levy some tolls and dues from the foreign vessels[11], without daring to come inland, except with a large force, wherewith however they never accomplished anything, except to despoil the country to their own hurt, and to lose a portion of their men, so that, on our arrival in these territories, they were not further occupied than a narrow strip of land, stretching from the islet of Poelian to the fisher's village named Cattencoedereripo, situated 3 hour's journey from there on the seashore[12]; and subsequently, when we handed over Batticalo to the King of Candi, we had before us a very dismal example, namely, that the King caused all these poor men to be carried off pitiably, and caused them for the most part to be put to death[13]. And since all the inhabitants of Batticalo (both in customs, religion, origin and other characteristics,) together with those of Jaffnapatnam, Cotjaar, and on westward right over to Calpentyn and the northern portion of the Mangul Corle inclusive, have been from the remotest times and are still now Malabaars, divided into their tribes, and very unwillingly mix with the Cingaleese, Weddas, or others outside their tribes, as also the others are not willing to do with these, they are up till now to be considered no otherwise than that they form with those of Jaffnapatnam, Cotjaar, &c. a people separate from the Cingaleese, and have up till now remained pretty well in their freedom; having accepted of their free will the Company's protection only in order to protect themselves against the cruelty of the King of Candi, wherefore it behoves us not to leave them in need or to delay if we do not wish to see them presently stand exposed to the

---

8. This statement, as to the semi-independence of the chiefs of the east coast territories, is corrobroated by the writers of the accounts of the first visits of the Dutch to Ceylon, given above.

9. Puliyantivu (see note 35 *infra*).

11. I have no details of these levies.

12. Káttánkuḍiyiruppu, now a large Moorish village, on the coast, 3½ miles south by east of Puliyantivu (Batticaloa town).

13. See Baldaeus, *Ceylon* xxi. (xxii. of Eng. trans.), and the accompanying realistic but fanciful plate.

same cruelty; since otherwise we have to expect from this rich, populous and fertile territory yet many fruits both temporal and spiritual.

This whole territory is not only very fertile, but also everywhere flat, and mostly clayey soil, excepting the shores, which are sandy, but nevertheless also fertile, and which are all mostly planted with *clappus*[14], *manggos*, *soorsaks*[15], and other useful trees, and further full of beautiful arable lands, meadows, and forests, that are watered by various rivers, all of which discharge into a large inland lake, that is quite 12 German miles long[16], and at its broadest 1 mile broad, and at its narrowest a musket shot wide, and wherein is so much fish, that, if matters were arranged therefore, one could transport from there yearly hundreds of lasts of salted fish, as commandeur de Graemme[17], (in order not to send the Company's yachts and shallops, of 20 and 35 lasts, empty to Colombo, whence he likewise requisitioned his wants) often did.

Nowhere in Ceylon is there more game, both of beasts and of birds, in the forests than in these territories, and nowhere also do the inhabitants, both rich and poor, eat rice, but here and in the [18]Corles in the west, situated right opposite thereto.

Cinnamon also grows here in super-abundance, and it was certainly exported from here yearly long before our occupation[19].

Nowhere in Ceylon is there more pepper, ginger, cardamom and other aromatic products, as also nowhere but here

---

14. Coconut (Malay *kelapa*).

15. Jak (see *Hobson-Jobson* s.v. " Soursop " *b*, and Wolf's *Life and Adventures* 126 for a quaint derivation of the name).

16. The lake is between 30 and 40 miles long.

17. In a previous part of ths document van Goens describes how this man, by a strange artifice, persuaded the Veddas to haul timber for him. A full plate depicts the incident.

18. This blank occurs in the original.

19. Tennent (ii. 34*n*.) quotes this statement (which he credits to Valentyn), and shows, on the authority of Dr. G. H. K. Thwaites, that cinnamon must once have grown extensively in the region round Batticaloa. See the statement of van Goens further on. I have found no reference to cinnamon in these parts in any of the Portuguese authorities.

is to be found in such super-abundance timber (although this is lacking nowhere in Ceylon); also nowhere are robuster and brave men, and in greater number, than here, so that they are in a position to repel all foreigners and inland enemies, being covered in the rear by the wild Weddas, so as not to be surprised by the highlanders, who could not approach them but from the direction of Panoa.

Thus one has everything that is distributed here and there over the whole of Ceylon here brought together briefly and concisely, whereby the Company will enjoy great profit herefrom, if we only remain 20 years free from European enemies[20].

The territories of Batticalo, which were also indeed named Mattacalappa[21], are divided [into] various provinces or small shires, and they were of old under three chiefs, either as *bandares*, who were appointed *dessaves* or Governors, either sovereign, or dependent on a higher one, or otherwise, and they are now still divided into three dessaveships, which we have now reduced to one (preserving, however the old division in names), namely Calare, Sjampanture, and Acrepatte[22]. The dessaveship of Calare is the principal and largest and has in it 4 provinces, named Mamone, Porredive, Errewielle, and Eraure[23].

Mamone consists of 11, Errewielle of 7, Porredive of 4, and Eraure of 5 large well peopled villages, besides many small hamlets, scattered in the rice-fields, and which with all their inhabitants are accurately described.

Especially noteworthy are the villages of Mamone, and still more so the chief village of Sjampanture, that is reckoned

---

20. The English and French had both made attempts (which had been frustrated by van Goens) to obtain a footing on Ceylon (see my *Captain Robert Knox* 13-14 and 25*n*. 11).

21. Sinh. Maḍakalapuwa, said to be from *mada*, mud, and *kalapuwa*, backwater; but the latter word seems to be undoubtedly of Tamil origin. H. Nevill (*Taprobanian* v. 141) thinks the first word should be *matti* (Sinh.), *mattai* (Tam),. 'cockle.'

22. Kallaru, Champanturai, and Akkarai Pattu.

23. Manmunai, Porativu Éruvil, and Eravur. In a map of Ceylon published by Joannes van Keulen about 1740, and said to have been drawn by order of Rijklof van Goens, the first two and the last provinces are named, but not Eruvil. The same is the case with a map of "The East Coast of Ceylon," published also by J. van Keulen about 1740.

to be quite 1½ hours' journey in length,[24] being situated on a fine river, at the passage where the *tsjanpans* arrive from the sea by the great backwater; and since the little word *ture* in Malabaars signifies a harbour, ferry, or place of arrival, it appears therefore to have obtained thence the name of Sjampanture[25], which kind of harbour, where the *tsjampans* arrive, is also found in the little district of Cotjaar[26].

And as I have myself travelled through this territory, I shall now describe it somewhat more particularly[27].

---

24. The village of Sammanturai consists at present of a small Tamil and a large Moorish division. In the map of Ceylon referred to in the previous note "Chiampanture" and "Motecaleppe" are shown adjoining each other, and in van Keulen's map of the east coast we find the same two names affixed to a huge enclosure, divided into two, and described as "Groote markt of handelplats" (great market or trading-place), outside of which is a small fort with the Dutch flag. This proves beyond a doubt that the town of "Matecalo" referred to by the first Dutch visitors to Ceylon was identical with Sammanturai, which was the residence of the "King of Matecalo" (see Spilbergen, Bree, and Ricks).

25. Mr Henry Parker writes to me:—"I am sorry that I cannot tell you much about Sammanturei (Sampanturai). The Sinhalese call it Hambantota, and the local tradition is that the water of the Batticaloa lake once extended up to the village. Since that time that end of the lake has silted up, a process still going on. The village is now some miles from the lake. It was certainly an ancient site, and there must have been a wihara near it in olden times. I saw some carved stones at the village which were said to have been removed from a site not far off. Two of these were the usual balustrades, with the *ali-honda* or elephant's trunk proceeding out of the mouth of a *makaran*. Another which I sketched is a triple-headed cobra in relief on an arched slab, which must have stood as a door guardian, at the end of the balustrade. There is also a pillar with fan, &c. and I think a dog and a crow engraved on it. but no inscription. You will find some particulars of Sammanturei in the 'Taprobanian,' vol. v, pp. 141-4." The article by Mr. Nevill is interesting, though not free from error, and shows the importance of the place in early times. That Sammanturai stood on the shore of the lake in the 17th century is proved by the statement of the Danish admiral Ove Giedde in his diary that in August, 1620, on returning from his embassy to Kandy, he obtained a "kanou" at "Siambandure," in which he proceeded to "Palligamme."

26. The reference seems to be to the village of Sammanturai in the Kottiyar Pattu of the Trincomalee district.

27. In his memorial of 26th December, 1663, handed to his successor Jacob Hustaert on vacating the governorship of Ceylon the first time, van Goens said of the territories extending from the Walawe-ganga to Trincomalee: "This territory I have never been able to travel through, it being wholly inhabited by the emperor's people; moreover a barren and dry land," &c. A better acquaintance with the region in question had shown him that he was entirely mistaken, so far as the northern portion was concerned.

The northernmost province Eraure borders on Tambancarrewarre, reaching to the bank of the river Nateoer, or to the inlet of Venlo's Bay, the border of the bank or west side of that backwater also belonging to this province from, Chittady Coedi Eripo [28] northward to the salt lake of Cockewille Polle[29] inclusive, so that Tambancarrewarre lies wedged between Cotjaar and Eraure; and this lake of Cockewille Polle and the great river of Mawielleganga lie scarcely 2 German miles from one another in a moorland and very marshy country, that could with little difficulty be dug through by the inhabitants, when one could sail through from the south from Accrepatte[30] as far as into the outer bay of Tricoenmale, and convey the timber, found in abundance in the territories of Batticalo, by this backwater right to the carpenter's shed. In this province is also found a very extensive cinnamon forest[31]. stretching in landwards, running through Welasse, and to all appearance as far as the west side in the Seven Corles, which here lie right opposite to and confine with each other[32]. This great forest is also full of fine timber, so that this province, on account both of its good situation and of its value, may certainly be placed amongst the best territories of Ceylon.

---

28. Sittandikuḍiyiruppu, near the Nattur lake, in Érávúr Pattu.

29. I cannot with certainty identify this "salt lake." J van Keulen's map of Ceylon of *circa*, 1740 shows "Koekevillepolle" as a village on the northern arm of a backwater entered by Venloos Bay, between "Tanmaquod" and "Tamboncarrewarre," but in Valentyn's map "'t Lak Cockewille Polle" is shown as a large inlet of the sea between "Cotjaar," and Tambancarrewarre." Perhaps Kankuvélikulum in Koṭṭiyàr Pattu is meant, "Polle" representing *paḷḷi* village.

30. The text in Valentyn has "Accepta."

31. Cf. note 19 *supra*. In a map of Venloos Bay, published by J. van Keulen about 1740, but drawn probably a good deal earlier, on the tract of land south of the bay is the notification "Hier wast wilde Caneel" (Here grows wild cinnamon).

32. Of course the Seven Korales do not confine with Wellassa, nor is it possible that the cinnamon jungle spoken of extended to anything like the distance supposed by the writer.

Next to this follow in order southwards Mamone[33], Porredive, and Errewille[34], which form the dessaveship of Calare[35].

These last three provinces occupy along the sea and along that backwater a distance at the least of 12 hours, and landwards 6 to 7 hours' journey as far as the wild forests of the Weddas, being all very fine and mostly fertile arable land, and further full of fruit-trees and timber, as also full of men, villages, and hamlets, from which one can very easily judge of the importance of the same.

The islet of Poelian[36] belongs with the adjacent island[37] to Mamone, lies about a cannon shot from the river inward, whereof the old Portuguese fortlet[38] has now been again entirely renewed with a small outwork,[39] and is also quite sufficient for the Company's convenience there, being very

---

33. Misprinted "Mancone."

34. See note 23 *supra*. Valentyn's map shows "Eraure," "Porredive" and "Errewille" as forming the dessaveship of "Calare," and "Mamone" by itself to the south of "Errewille." The positions of the provinces are very incorrect.

35. Misprinted "Elare."

36. Puliyantivu (see Introd. note 36 and note 38 infra). H. Nevill (*Taprobanian* v. 141) spells the name with an ordinary *l*, and derives the name from a certain Puliyan. He also says, not quite correctly :—"The silting up and elevation of the lagoon, having caused ships to anchor far north, near Puliyantivu, Puliyantivu has acquired the old port's name of Mattakalapu or Batticaloa, amongst European and native sailors, but not amongst people of the province."

37. Buffalo Island.

38. This "fortlet" was built in 1627 by Constantino de Sá, according to his son in his *Rebelion de Ceylon* xi (see C. A. S. Jl. xi. 566-7, where, however, the translation is faulty). But in the *Livro do Estado da India Oriental* compiled in 1646 by Pedro Barretto de Ressende (B. M. Sloane Ms. 197), it is stated that this was built by Damiam. Botado in 1628 during the captain-generalship of Constantino de Sá. (This is confirmed by Baldaeus, who tells us that Botado was a mixty —*cf.* pp. 44*c* and 44*g* of his *Ceylon*). The Ressende MS. contains a coloured plan of the fort, which corresponds pretty exactly with the plan given by Baldaeus (*Ceylon* 55), except that in the latter the position is reversed. The Ressende MS. gives a detailed description of the fort, its ordnance, garrison, &c., and Baldaeus gives a brief description in chap. xxii. of Eng. trans). Ribeiro also, in his *Fatalidade Historica* I. xii., has a short account of the fort.

39. Valentyn, at p. 32 of his *Ceylon*, gives a plan of Batticalo fort by "T. C. Worzee, Ingenieur," dated, 4th July, 1698, which shows the alterations made at that period, a fourth bastion having taken the place of the old Portuguese *couraça*. The description of the fort given on p. 32 is taken (without acknowledgment) from Baldaeus, and does not correspond with the plate.

easily capable of being defended in time of peace by 25 men; but the air here is heavy, and very unwholesome, owing to the adjacent pools and marshes; the drinking water and fuel also have to be brought from outside[40], which is very inconvenient for the capital of a province of such importance, wherefore, having looked out for a healthier and better place, one has found best the point of Soratjan Candave[41], close to the shore, near a little inlet, in the middle of the territory, close by an ever outflowing fresh river[42], and supplied within with very fine fresh water, as also of a high ground, and free, wholesome air, as good as anywhere else in Ceylon, the very finest villages standing around it on the land side[43], as it is also so convenient to the sea, that one can very easily lie there (without any surf) with large and small vessels, and step out dryfooted on to a jetty; and what in addition results very fortunately is, that the ships could lie here the whole south season right under the weather shore with a bad sea, scarcely a musket shot from the shore, as well as before the fort of Jaffnapatnam[44].

Here dwell the most people, and all building materials, such as stone, lime, firewood, and everything else, are here in abundance at the shore, and hereby also the whole strip of

---

40. Baldaeus (*u. s.*) states that it was the seizure of the water supply by the Dutch that forced the Portuguese garrison to capitulate.

41. What this name represents, it is not easy to tell. But of its situation there is little doubt. Valentyn enters it in his map; but the latter teems with errors, and no reliance can be placed in it. Curiously enough, H. van Keulen's map of Ceylon of *circa* 1740 does not contain the name; but his map of the east coast of Ceylon has "Sorotjancondave" at a point forming a bay to the north in 7° 10½′ N. This latitude is incorrect, however, for the place lies between "Lansimaradarey" (Saintamarutu) and "Panicoewetavi" (Panichchavattaván): so that it must be located in the vicinity of Karativu, which lies in about 7° 20½′ N. This location corresponds with the details given by the writer and the distance mentioned by him further on (see note 50). In Nicolaus Visscher's map of Ceylon (? 1680-1725) is the entry, south of "Chanchimadre" (Saintamorutu), "Sorotjan Codowe, een Kleyn Baaytje om te landen" (S. C., a little bay for landing).

42. A branch of the Gal-oya flows into a small backwater near Karativu.

43. Among them Sammanturai, to which a road leads direct from Karativu.

44. What amount of truth there is in these sanguine statements, I am unable to say.

land on the east side of the backwater or lake is protected, and cut off from the mainland[45].

What kind of fortifications could be built there, can be seen in the accompanying map[46], which in time could be completed without any appreciable expense owing to the abundance of requisites.

Bricks can also here be baked in abundance, which is already carried on by the potters; and in conformity with the division of the sea-shore[47] a hardy walker should be able to go in one day from here to the river of Coeboucan-oye[48], where our Gale lascaryns, it being the end of the Gale jurisdiction, always keep watch; whence an ordinary walker can easily get in three days to Mature, and in four days reach Gale, as also now already letters are brought through from watch to watch divided into six hours' journey.

Most of our men are now always garrisoned at Cinnecalatte[49], 2 miles north of Souratjan Condava[50], who after the effectuation of the new chief residency would in no wise be

---

45. At that period the Batticaloa lake extended as far south as Sammanturai (see note 25 supra).

46. Whether this map is still extant, or, like van Goen's original memorial, has perished, I cannot say.

47. That is, the division made by the Dutch for its defence.

48. The Kumbukkan-aru, or Kumbukgam-oya, which forms the boundary between the Eastern and Southern Provinces. The distance from Karativu by the present coast road is 68¼ miles.

49. J. van Keulen's map of Ceylon has "Cinneklattedelle" located erroneously, the compiler having misunderstood the name as representing the village of Kallodi, half-a-mile south-east-by-south of Puliyantivu, and placing it accordingly. (In consequence of this error other places have been wrongly located.) In his map of the east coast of Ceylon, however, van Keulen shows "Chinnecalette," much further south, on a little island in the Batticaloa lake, close to the sea, with a fort flying the Dutch flag, south of it being "Periecalette." It is evident that by this last name is meant Periyakallaru, and that the former name represents Chinnakallâru, now Kóttaikkallâru, so called from the fort mentioned. Another small map of van Keulen's shows the fort of "Ciri Calattedelle" (Sinnakallarruveli ?) right on the seashore, and to the south a little bay with the curious name "Sioetanterloedan" from which is drawn a line due east and west to the Friar's Hood, which is shown in the background. Sailing directions from coming into "Civi Calatte delle" are appended.

50. According to the scales on van Keulen's maps, 2 German miles = about 2¾ English or French leagues; so that "Souratjan Condava" should be about 8 miles south of Kottaikkallaru. Karativu is 9 miles from the latter place. (Cf. note 40 supra).

needed there, but could be placed in this new fortification[51].

The second dessaveship consists of the provinces of Sjampanture and Carrewauwe[52], the latter being situated on the sea, and all mostly arable lands and fruit-trees, forming thus a fine open country; but Sjampanture extends quite 8 to 9 miles inland, full of arable lands, great forests, and flowing rivers, everywherè studded with large and small habitations of men.

Next to these two follows the province of Accrepatte, or the third dessaveship, having its beginning with the river of Singanpoedi[53] in the north, as far as the gravet of Sangamcandi in the south, being the limit of the Batticaloa territories, and the entrance to the territories of Paneme, otherwise called Panoa by the Cingaleese[54].

This is likewise, not less than Sjampanture, a very large and rich province, extending far inland as far as the gravets of Welasse and the territories of the Weddas, very full of men, and such fine forests, arable lands, villages and hamlets, that one cannot look at it without wonder; so that this last Batticalo dessaveship may well be esteemed as the first.

Here also stands the *pagode* of Tricoen entered in the map as Tricoyl, this Tricoen being a certain Malabaarish idol, who is invoked for success at sea, and in agriculture, as Tricoyl signifies no other than "Tricoen's temple," and Tricoen-male "Tricoen's mount.[55]"

The inhabitants are all Malabaars, just like those of Jaffanapatnam and Cotjaar; but are said to be somewhat

---

51. For some reason unknown to me van Goens's proposed transfer of the Dutch garrison and seat of government of the east coast territories from "Baticalo" to "Soratjan Condava" did not take effect. I have found no other allusion to the subject.

52. Karaiváku Pattu. Neither of van Keulen's maps referred to above has this name. The maps of Nicolaus Visscher and others have "Carrewarre" as a town or village on the coast north of "Chanchimadre" (Saintawarutu), and Valentyn's map (copied by Isaac Tirion) has the same place as "Carrewauwe."

53. The Sangapada or Sengalpadai-aru, a branch of the Gal-oya.

54. Pánama or Pánawa.

55. All this is, of course, very incorrect. Tirukkovil means simply "Sacred temple" (though it might mean "temple of Tiru," the goddess of prosperity), and it is dedicated to Skanda, the god of war (cf. what the Spilbergen diarist relates, *supra*). Trincomalee is a corruption of Tirukonathamalai, "hill of the sacred Konatha."

more ill-natured, and knavish owing to their intercourse with the Cingaleese, Môors, and others : because thus far did the dominion of the old Malabaarish rajas extend, and so along the high mountain range and the territories of the Weddas right over to Putelam and the middle of Calpentyn or Navecar[56], it being further expanded to the southward under their control along the sea-coast on the west side as far as Nigombo, and on the east side as far as Paneme and the river of Coeboucan Oye, when even now ordinarily nothing but Malabaarish is spoken (although they also understand Cingaleese) ; and because the Cingaleese language from here southwards does not begin before one crosses the river Coeboucan Oye in the east and comes into the Mangul Corle[57] on the west, and the territories of Panoa seem to belong most properly to the Malabaarish division, they have by your honors confirmation been placed under the Batticalo *commandement*, because the territory and the people are entirely in unison with those of Accrepatte, are intermarried, and have one language and customs, although they used to be subject to a separate rule ; but now to their particular satisfaction taken, with those of the Batticalo territories, under the Company's protection.

The district of Panoa is found to differ markedly from the Batticalo territories, both in fertility and especially in men ; however, from the gravet of Sangamcondi to the large village of Arrockgamme[58] it is very fertile, and as full of men

56. Nawakkadu in the Akkrai Pattu of the Puttalam district, at the south-western end of the Puttalam lake (*cf. M. Lit. Reg.* iv. 157 *n.*§).

57. The Mangul (Magul) Kóralé (regarding which see Casie Chitty's *Gazatteer*) no longer exists as a separate division but is represented by the Magul Ọṭọ́ṭà Kóralé and the Magul Medagandahé Kóraḷé East and West of the Vanni Hatpattu, Kurunegala district, N.W.P.

58. Potuwiḷa is doubtless meant, which is a large Tamil and Sinhalese village just north of Aragam *Kalapuwa* and bay. This bay is entered in J. van Keulen's map of Ceylon as " de baey van Aoebgamme" with a village on the northern point. Casie Chitty's *Gazetteer* (as corrected by him for a new edition, never published) has :—" *Arrookgam,* a [*large and populous*] village of Panoa Pattoo, about 64 miles [*east*] south of Batticalo, situated on the bay of the same name, and encompassed on the land side by thick jungles, the resort of all sorts of game. It was once occupied by the Dutch Government as a military post, and had a small mud fort ; but [*now there is only a large store house, in which the paddy tithes collected in this part of the country are deposited*] is now deserted except by wood cutters, and a few, Singhalese Dhoneys on their way home at the end of the south-west monsoon."

as in the case of the Batticalo territories ; but from Arrockgammie southwards the territory is more sparsely inhabited and cultivated.

Half-an-hour's journey south of Arrockgamme lies the harbour of Appretotte[59], where it is thought that a redoubt would come in very well. to secure our property and the inhabitants there, it being of a particularly good situation, in that the hookers can lie there in a rough sea so close to the shore, that one can go out of them by a plank. Moreover there is here nothing to fear as to coming in there during the whole of the south and north *moesson*, as one also can easily come here from the north the whole year through, and so also depart again to the north, which in the south season can be done with great difficulty more to the south or west, except here, because the land here begins to fall off more westerly.

If this place of arrival were only secured with a redoubt, the whole of Batticalo and Panoa would be protected, which therefore also ought to be made the sooner the better, as has several times been represented to your honors.

---

59. " Appretotte Bay " is to be found on maps of Ceylon and, Admiralty Charts down to quite recent times ; but there is a mystery about the name that I have not solved. In N. Visscher's map of Ceylon it does not appear ; but in J. van Keulen's map " Approeretotte " is shown as a village on the southern point of the bay of " Aoebgamme " (see previous note). There is also a large scale map of van Keulen's with the following title (translated) :—" Chart of the bay of Aproeretotte situated at the north-east angle of the district of Panoa or Paneme, in the island of Ceylon, under 6 degrees 45 min., but according to the saying of others under 6 degrees 55 min., 16 ordinary, that is, about 14 true German miles south of the entrance to the river of, Baticalo." This shows a bay, with an inner *Kalapuwa* into which fall several rivers or streams. At the northern point of the bay is a cliff, and the name " Aoebgamme." At the southern point of the bay is another cliff, and the name " Aproeretotte." On the north side of the *Kalapuwa* is a peaked hill, and on a point running into the *Kalapuwa* on the south is a rocky mound. Beside a stream that runs into the *Kalapuwa* at its western side is the name " Agasum or Agaus." (This last name is also found in fairly recent maps and charts, with the variant spellings " Aganis " and " Agais.") Taking all things into consideration, it seems almost certain that " Appretotte Bay " is Aragam Bay under another name. (Cf. Casie Chitty's statement, quoted in the previous note, as to the existence of a Dutch fort there). And I cannot help suspecting that " Appretotte " is a " ghost " name, evolved from the Tamil *appurutturei*, " beyond the ferry." " Agasum" appears as a village north of " Mandagale " in Gerard van Keulen's map of Ceylon (circa. 1720), and on Thomas Bowrey's map of the island drawn in 1681 is " Agaijun ; " but I do not find the name on other maps.

These territories of Panoa used also to have a dessave over them, and if he was one of their fellow-countrymen the Cingaleese Kings got on best; as otherwise they used very readily and frequently to revolt, and to flee to the provinces of Acurepatte.

How far landward their limits are, has not yet been investigated; but according to the report made to us, the Cingaleese within the uplands could reach them quickly; so that it appears that to the south of Apretotte they could not be freed inwardly so well as could the Batticalo territories by means of the Weddas, and therefore used now and then to be subjected to the inroads of the Cingaleese.

For many years now on the other hand one has found these Panoars, above others of these regions, very devoted to us, so that, to our great wonder, they are not only obedient to us, but also so faithful, that they, as well as those of the Batticalo territories, come to present themselves at their proper time to fulfil their obligations, also bringing our letters right over to Colombo. And as soon as any rumour comes from above, our people, both at Mature and at Batticalo, are at once warned and our protection sought by them. They also will not desist from asking, until we have placed there a redoubt with 18 to 20 of our men, which connot be done entirely without expense to the hon. Company, but which will also conduce to great security of the lowlands, and serve as a southern frontier for the border of the seashores, round about the island, and for the Batticalo territories in particular.

THE EARLIEST DUTCH VISITS TO CEYLON.

BY DONALI FERGUSON.

Continued from Vol. XXI, No. 81, p. 379.

THE SOUTH-EAST COAST OF CEYLON.

REMARKABLE HILLS AND OTHER LANDMARKS.

(From Imray's "Indian Ocean Pilot," pp. 893-4, 897-8).

The south-east coast of Ceylon between Dorava [1] and Julius Nave [2] points, a space of 30 miles, trends nearly N.E. and S.W., with ranges of high mountains inland, often obscured, however, by the hazy state of the atmosphere, said to be peculiar to this part of the island, particularly during the south-west monsoon.

Near the coast inside the line of the Basses, are several hills of remarkable form, which from their position are admirable landmarks, during daylight and fine weather, for navigating in the vicinity of the Basses.

The shore is comparatively low and barren, fringed with a belt of sand, but without any marked salient features; the points are generally rounded and sandy, rising to elevations of about 100 feet. Off the pitch of all the points are rocky patches, extending in some cases a quarter of a mile. Along the whole line of coast the surf breaks heavily on the beach, the first roller rising at the average distance of a cable from the shore.

1. Dorawa is between Mágama and Kirinda.
2. This name is found on some of the olden maps of Ceylon: I do not know the origin. Judging by the distance named, apparently Mahagajabuwa, just south of the Kumbukkan-áru, is intended.

Kattregamme Hill.—The most prominent land seen when approaching the Basses from the westward is the Kattregamme range of hills, the nearest and highest of which is 7 or 8 miles from the sea. These hills are sometimes conspicuous both from eastward and westward, when others nearer the sea are hardly discernible. Their summit presents an irregular ridge, the north-east peak of which is the highest, being 1,972 feet [3] above the sea.

Elephant Hill, the next height to the eastward, is conspicuous as it stands alone on the low land near the shore, and bears a remarkable resemblance to the animal from which it is named. It is two miles from the beach and bare of trees on its summit, which is 480 feet above the sea.

Little Elephant Hill, in shape resembling a hay cock, stands on the extreme point forming the western horn of Elephant bay. It is 105 feet high, and from it Elephant hill bears N.W. ½ N. distant two miles.

* * * *

Nipple Hill, farther inland than the other hills, bears from Elephant hill N. by E. ¾ E. distant about 9 miles. Rendered conspicuous by its superior elevation, 903 feet above the sea, which places it as if above, this peak is also distinguished by a flattened summit, with two lumps (one at each end) in a direction about W.S.W. and E.N.E., from which it derives its name ; the western of these nipples is the higher. This hill may also be known by a remarkable cone W.S.W. from it, which is generally distinguishable, but more so when viewed from eastward, although it is only 520 feet above the sea.

Chimney Hill, next in succession eastward, is of much service to a vessel for ascertaining her position in reference to the Basses. It is 4½ miles from the nearest beach, 445 feet [4] above the sea, and very conspicuous,

3. The height of Kataragama Peak is actually 1,395 feet.
4. The heights given for this and the foregoing hills I cannot verify.

being the highest part of a low range, which takes an east and west direction; it appears to be separated from the western part of the range, and derives its name from its resemblance to a chimney. From the Great Basses it is not easily seen, being in fact sometimes entirely concealed by the haze which generally hangs over the land, especially during the south-west monsoon.

* * * *

From Julius Nave point the coast trends N.N.E. nearly 20 miles to Appretotte point [5] in about lat. 6° 47′ N., long. 81° 50′ 45″ E., and then 15 miles N. ¾ E. to Shanghe-man-kande [6] point, in lat. 7° 2′ 10″ N., long. 81° 53′ E., the most eastern projection of Ceylon. On the south side of Appretotte point is the mouth of Naveloor river [7]; and, on the north side, that of the Chadewakke. [8]

At about 3 miles north of it is Abrookgam [9] bay, of which nothing is known further than that it is the outlet of a stream [10] of no great magnitude that flows through the country around Lion peak. [11] The land hereabouts is named Aganis [12] in old charts. It is low, with sandy hillocks near the shore. In the interior, at about 12 miles from the sea, and W. N. W. from Appretotte point, there is an isolated hill 821 feet high, which appears peaked when viewed from eastward, but notched when seen from southward; hence it is known as the Saddle hill. Lion peak, 956 feet high, [13] is also conspicuous from the offing; it is 20 miles from the nearest shore, and readily recognised by its form, that of a lion *couchant*. Westminster Abbey,

---

5. Gónáduwa. On "Appretotte," see G 3, note 59.
6. Sangamakanda.
7. The Nával-áru.
8. The Chedawak-áru, or Heda-oya.
9. See G 2, note 58.
10. The Arukgam-áru, or Karanda-oya
11. See further on.
12. See G 2, note 59.
13. I cannot verify the heights given for this and the preceding hill.

a table mountain 1,258 feet high,[14] and a few miles farther in the interior than Lion peak, will be distinguished without difficulty, as it has on its north end a large square knob resembling a turret. Aganis peak,[15] nearly midway between Westminster Abbey and the coast, is 767 feet high, and from seaward is in line with that mountain on the bearings of W. ½ S. These comprise the most prominent landmarks in the interior of the south-eastern part of Ceylon, south of lat. 7° 10′ N., then after some miles follow the Friar's Hood (Wallingbehella) in lat. 7° 26½′ N., long. 81° 28¼′ E., a mountain 1,563 feet high[16] and about 20 miles from the sea, which, from the circumstance that it leans over to the left, resembles a friar's hood when bearing to the S. W., but a pyramid when to the N.W. Southward from this a short distance, is another mountain of less height, and somewhat like it, which is known as the False Friar's Hood. The Kettle-bottom, 1,190 feet high, is a round conical hill in lat. 7° 32′ N., long. 81° 13¼′ E., it is 16 miles from Friar's Hood on the bearing of W.N.W. ¼ W. The Sugar-loaf, 24 miles northward from Friar's Hood and 14 miles from the sea, is 532 feet high.[17] Farther in the interior, on the bearing of W. ⅔ N., is the Gunner's Quoin, having an estimated height of 1,320 feet.[18] And, a few miles more to the northward, but nearer the sea, are two smaller mountains, known as the Baron's Cap and the Small Quoin, of which the latter is nearest the coast. The Baron's Cap is 473 feet high,[19] 11 miles from the shore, and nearly midway between Batticaloa river and Trincomalie bay.

---

14. The correct height of Westminster Abbey Hill is 1,830 feet.
15. I cannot identify this.
16. The true height of Friar's Hood is 2,148 feet.
17. I cannot verify the heights of this and the preceding hill.
18. The actual height is 1,736 feet.
19. The real height of the Baron's Cap is 691 feet, and that of the Small Quoin is 524 feet.

From Shangheman-kande point the coast sweeps round to the N. ¾ W., and at 13 miles we meet with the Singare-topu-aar.[20] a barred river, southward of which at a place called Tricoll,[21] there is a pagoda, in a grove of cocoa-nut trees. Between the point and the river, several small streams enter the sea by very shallow mouths. It then trends N. by W. ¾ W. 30 miles to Batticaloa river. All the land is low near the sea, and there are numerous plantations of cocoa-nut trees in proximity to the shore, besides a few villages. Near Batticaloa the coast is very low.

20. I do not know what name this represents. From the distance given, apparently the Tampodai backwater is meant.
21. Tirukkóvil (see D 2, note 101).